THE THREE CHOIRS WAY

'I have tried to define and
express what it meant to me,
a potential musician, nurtured
in countryside of companionable
hills, two lovely but diverse rivers
and three magnificent cathedrals.
It seems that Severn and Wye
flow through one's veins …
and the astonishing Three Choirs
Festivals go their historic way.'

Herbert Howells

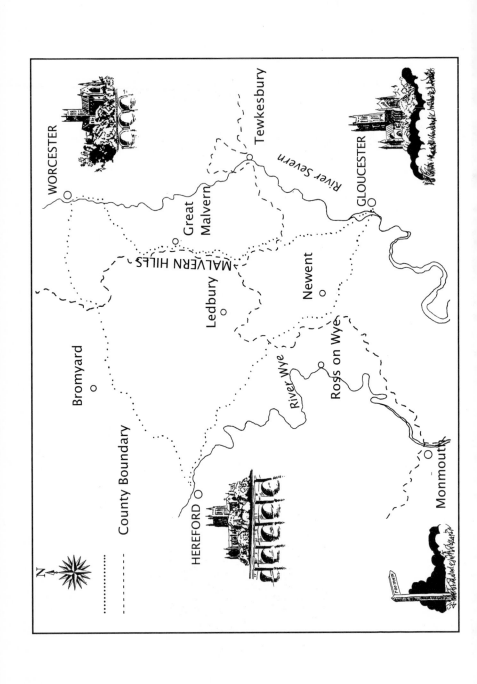

THE THREE CHOIRS WAY

Only the wanderer
  Knows England's graces,
Or can anew see clear
  Familiar faces

And who loves joy as he
  That dwells in shadows?
Do not forget me quite
  O Severn meadows.

Ivor Gurney

Designed and compiled by
Gerry Stewart

COUNTRYSIDE MATTERS

Published in 1999 by
COUNTRYSIDE MATTERS
15 Orchard Road
Alderton
Tewkesbury
Gloucestershire   GL20 8NS

Typeset by Ex Libris Press
Bradford on Avon, Wiltshire

Printed and bound by Cromwell Press
Trowbridge, Wiltshire

© Gerry Stewart 1999

ISBN 09527870 2 4

Contents

Credits

The Publishers wish to express their thanks for the use of the following poems which enhance the Three Choirs Way. While every effort has been made to contact all copyright holders, the publishers would be pleased to hear from anyone whom they have been unable to trace.

Penny Ely, Trustee of the Gurney Estate, for *'Song'*, by Ivor Gurney, from *'The collected Poems'*.
Alan Holden, for *'Worcestershire Lanes'*, by Molly Holden, from *'Selected Poems 1987'*.
Jeffrey Cooper for *'Ryton Firs'*, by Lascelles Abercrombie, from *'Twelve Idylls'*.
Geoffrey Bright, for *'On Croft Ambury'*, from *'Hereford is Heaven'*.
Robert Wade for *'The Wye at Hereford'*, from *'Verses'*.
Geoffrey Mason for *'Carpenters'*.
Robin Ivy for *'Severn'*, from *'Worcestershire Suite 1992'*.

Acknowledgements

In 1989, Geoff Emms wrote, in Tewkesbury Walking Club's Newsletter, *"Over the past three years the Club has celebrated the Three Choirs Festival with combined walks and visits to performances in the three cathedral cities - Worcester 1987, Hereford 1988 and a grand finale this year at Gloucester"*

The grand finale he referred to was a weekend of walks, with a theme of local poetry and music, which Kate and myself arranged on both sides of the Severn, and which culminated with a visit to a concert at Gloucester cathedral. Geoff added *"Inside, the evening sunlight flooded through the stained glass windows to provide a fitting backcloth for Elgar at his best. Even the bats joining in the performance"*.

This book, a further attempt to enhance the pleasures of cross country walking with a flavour of music and poetry, arose from the events which Geoff and Joy inaugurated ten years ago. In appreciation of their enthusiasm and the innovative pleasures which they generated for their fellow walkers, the Three Choirs Way is for them.

My thanks are also due again to my daughter, Genny Proctor, for many of the illustrations on the cover and elsewhere in the book.

My wife Kate has again staunchly supported the venture. Beyond car shuttles and wet and muddy walks in the dim reaches of Herefordshire, she has borne the brunt of proof reading, sometimes stressfully, as when she felt it necessary to delete some of my more bucolic prose.

My thanks also to the various friends who helped on the first probing walks for a feasible route. In particular, Margaret and Graham Davies, George Gilbody and Peter Collins strove through part of the wettest winter for eighty years checking the route description and correcting a few flaws in the process.

Author's Note

Changes continually take place in the countryside, hedges disappear, new fences, sometimes without stiles or gates, arise and paths may be difficult to follow through crops. Also, public rights of way are subject to legal diversions which may not be reflected in current maps. The County Council's signposting should reveal any changes but the situation may not always be clear on the ground.

The Three Choirs Way is predominantly along public highways, mainly footpaths and bridleways. Variations occur, and where stiles, gates and bridges are not in the correct spot for some reason, these are used for obvious convenience. Permissive paths are also used where they are preferable to the right of way, for instance along the Lugg at Mordiford and on the Malvern Hills, where numerous permissive paths complement the many public rights of way.

The sketch maps are quite adequate for the walk, but many, particularly strangers to the area, will want to relate to the surrounding countryside. The OS Landranger, 149, 150 and 162, or the new Explorer series, provide wider detail.

Although the Three Choirs Way is described clockwise from Gloucester it can of course be commenced from Hereford or Worcester, or many places in between, and in either direction. Likewise, although I have set out sections of about 12 miles, this is arbitrary, and 10 mile sections or even shorter, circular links, can be devised. The mileage chart will assist individual planning. Pubs, mostly serving food, occur at regular intervals and many of the villages still have shops.

Public transport connects the three cities but is much more difficult to co-ordinate in between. Mini buses or coaches, hired according to the size of the party, offer an economic way to the start or finish of the sections. Many pubs will permit parking if you are likely to patronise the premises and church wardens will often permit parking, where available, as at Woolhope, Withington, Much Cowarne etc. in return for a contribution to Church funds.

It should be particularly noted that in the winter months the low lying areas near the rivers at Gloucester, Worcester and Hereford can be severely affected by flooding. The only option then may be wide detours on alternative paths or, even more inconveniently, along adjacent roads.

Whilst great care has been taken to ensure that the information provided in this book is accurate, neither the author nor publisher can accept responsibility for any errors or omissions or for the interpretation of the information by users of this guide book.

Introduction

The origins of the Three Choirs Festival were very informal, and it was probably the nearness of the three cities to each other that gave rise to friendly and unceremonious gatherings of the individual musical clubs. In 1719, *'The Worcester Postman'* reported *"the yearly musical assembly of these parts, held last year in Gloucester, will meet at Worcester on the last day of August"*.

The cathedrals were traditionally the centres of musical interest, and combined choral services were a natural outcome of popular local interest in good music.

In 1720, in a sermon given to the anniversary meeting of the Worcester, Gloucester and Hereford choirs, the Chancellor of Hereford Cathedral, Dr Thomas Bisse, proposed that at future meetings a collection be taken up for the benefit of the widows and orphans of clergy. As a result from 1724 the previous informality became more purposeful, and the Festivals were organised formal events.

Music Festivals are popular throughout Britain and Europe, some, such as Bath and Cheltenham are of recent origin, but others have faded from memory. The continuity of the Three Choirs Festival of Hereford, Worcester and Gloucester, is unique, since it began before the birth of Haydn, Mozart and Beethoven, and not long after the deaths of Handel and Bach, it has the distinction of being the oldest musical festival in Europe. The list of composers such as Elgar, Holst, Vaughan Williams, Berkeley, Walton, Bliss, Britten and Finzi, is impressive.

Of many anecdotes that accord pleasantly in a walking book, an apt story is that of Gustav Holst, who arrived at Gloucester cathedral, to conduct a choral rehearsal, soaking wet from the knees down. Apparently he had walked 'an ancient Roman trackway' to reach the cathedral. No doubt walkers of the Three Choirs Way will readily sympathise with him.

The Three Choirs Festival has brought fame to some composers there, and there can be little doubt that the countryside of the three counties has been an inspiration to many of them, whether born or who have chosen to live in the area.

The Gloucestershire composer, Herbert Howells has written that *'the festivals are too parochial'*, apparently an overheard remark, but which he claimed has an element of historic truth...

"I have tried to define and express what it meant to me, a potential musician, nurtured in countryside of companionable hills, two lovely but diverse rivers and three magnificent cathedrals. It seems that Severn and Wye flow through one's veins... and the astonishing Three Choirs Festivals go their historic way".

He lucidly expresses the sentiments of what the Three Choirs Way is intended to be, and I hope that you too will experience this.

On Croft Ambury

I climbed the hill where many years ago,
  The Ancient Briton made his final stand,
And gazing at the wondrous scene below,
  Thanked him who made this lovely, peaceful land.
For far as eye could travel, were the hills,
  The streams, the woods, the rich red soil,
The verdant fields, the babbling hurrying rills,
  The age-long fight of Nature 'gainst man's toil.

Far to the West, the broken line of Wales,
  Was marked by Hergest, Hanter and the Gore;
Like galleons rigged with square top-gallant sails,
  To garner fickle winds that blow off shore;
And nearer was the long Silurian ridge,
  That runs past lovely Ludlow to the Clees,
With Wopley, Shobdon, Bircher, Wenlock Edge,
  Gatley and high Vinnals with its trees.

And to the East, as if they stand on guard,
  The Malverns rising from the Severn's plain;
And Hegdon Hill that lies beyond Bromyard,
  And in the valley Leominsters Norman fane;
And softly, grey against the dark green trees,
  Of Eaton Hill, and Dinmore's wooded slope,
The smoke that wafted slowly in the breeze,
  Marked Leominster Town, Stoke Prior and Hope.

And further to the South I could discern,
  Beyond the glorious valley of the Wye,
Lone Garway's coloured coat of gorse and fern,
  And May Hill's clump of firs against the sky;
And Skirrid's Holy Mountain, with the rift
  That gives distinction to that pointed height,
And nestling at the foot of Ladylift,
  Old Weobley's patch of chequered black and white.

And then I saw the grandest of them all,
A massive line of blue, and black, and grey,
Black Mountains, running like a wall
From Pandy and Pontrillas up to Hay:
Where once King Arthur and his valiant knights,
On evenings when the mountain air was still,
Pursued the wild deer upon these heights,
Or sat at leisured ease on Merbach Hill.

Then far beyond the border town of Hay,
Naked and gaunt, without a single tree,
The Brecknock Beacons seemed to bar the way
To Pembroke, and the stormy Irish Sea.
And as I gazed, I slipped into the past,
And thought I saw a cavalcade
Of men in armour, riding very fast;
Wild Welshmen on a border raid.

And now the magic circle was complete,
Except for hills that flanked the silvery Wye;
The Eppynts with their little fields so neat,
Like coloured patchwork quilts, hung out to dry.
And there, within this ring of noble heights,
The varied hues of nature in accord,
With boundless sky, and ever changing lights,
The pleasant fertile land of Hereford.

                              Geoffrey Bright
(From Hereford is Heaven)

13

Gloucester to Kilcot

Until the building of the Severn bridges, Gloucester was, for centuries, the major crossing point of the Severn, an ancient frontier and centre for trade. The Romans early established a fort and Glevum became a place of retirement for officers and administrators. Wherever a hole is dug in the city it is said that 2000 years of occupation will be found.

Following the Romans and Saxons, the Normans commenced work on the cathedral, the tower, 225 feet high, is a landmark clearly seen for many miles.

In 1089 William the Conqueror ordered the preparation of Doomsday Book from his parliament in Gloucester.

Edward II, murdered at nearby Berkeley, was entombed in the cathedral which resulted in its becoming a place of pilgrimage. The prosperity which followed provided the 3000 inhabitants with a total of five monasteries and twelve churches, giving rise, later in history, to Shakespeare's comment "as sure as God's in Gloucester".

Unfortunately, the city elders backed Cromwell in the Civil War withstanding a determined and expensive siege by the Kings forces in 1643. On his restoration the King sought his dues and caused the city walls, which would have been the equal of York or Chester today, to be demolished.

Modern road construction has obliterated much of the mediaeval causeway from Westgate out of the city, and a direct route to Telford's bridge no longer exists.

From the Cathedral walk down Westgate Street to reach the River Severn. A pedestrian flyover is the better option for crossing the inner ring-road and a pedestrian bridge avoids the traffic crossing the eastern arm of the river. Then follow an underpass right and left to a footway outside cottages at Pool Meadow.

Ignore Severn Way signposts and walk away from the river for 100 yards to a gate and stile on the right, the start of a quiet route, shared with the *Gloucestershire Way* out of the city. Follow a track through parkland to another gate and walk under the railway viaduct. Turn left along the boundary of a sports field, *Gloucester Irish Associations Hurling Pitch,* and cross a stile and footbridge.

Pass beneath the pillars of the flyover to a footbridge and cross the water meadow to the grass ramp to Telford's Bridge spanning the west channel of the Severn. An English Heritage site, the bridge is pleasantly isolated from the nearby rush of traffic and already provides passage for the Wysis Way and the Gloucestershire Way.

The Wysis Way runs for 55 miles, through the Forest of Dean, Severn Vale and Cotswold, linking Offa's Dyke Path on the Wye at Monmouth, to the Thames Path at Kemble. Providing 400 miles of walking from the North Wales coast to Greenwich.

The Gloucestershire Way is a continuous path of 100 miles from Chepstow to Tewkesbury, passing through Gloucester and Stow on the Wold and Winchcombe. The walk provides a link between several long distance routes from Offas's' Dyke Path to the Cotswold Way, Oxfordshire Way, and Heart of England Way.

Designed by Thomas Telford and copied from a bridge over the Seine it was opened in 1831. The arch is a graceful ellipse enhanced by the chamfering of the stonework to ease the flow of floodwaters. A keen eye will detect where the crown of the arch sank considerably when the scaffolding was first removed. No doubt a heart stopping moment for the masons and engineers, but Telford is said to have expected it! The bridge replaced a 13th century structure described by the historian Leland... a seven arch stone bridge nearest the city, then one of five arches, followed by 'the great causey of stone forced up through the low meads of Severne' and finally a bridge of eight arches.

Leaving the bridge turn left, with the *Wysis Way*, and cross the dual carriageway, passing the Dog Inn, and turn into Lassington Lane alongside Over Farm shop. Follow the lane for over half a mile until it bends left and then climb a stile into Lassington Wood. There are several ways through the wood, not all rights of way. Follow a right fork which rises to the wood edge. Cross two stiles in succession, then walk diagonally left to a further stile at the roadside.

Nearby is Highnam Court, where Thomas Gambier Parry was often host to notable composers including Elgar and Vaughan Williams. His son Hubert had his first success as a composer, with 'Prometheus Unbound', at the Gloucester Festival of 1880. Hubert's lectures, on the history of music, later enthralled Holst and Vaughan Williams, but his major fame is for the music to Blakes immortal 'Jerusalem'.

Walk down the wide grass verge to an area of young trees and fork right down to a stile and into a narrow field. At the far end cross a stile and turn left over a further stile alongside a gate, and walk down the track to a lane.

Turn right, bending left, to Lassington Court and the disused church. *Originally Saxon, the Church was dedicated on Palm Sunday 1095 AD.* Turn left between farm buildings and follow the bridleway track across the field, turning right and then left along the edge of woodland before descending to a bridle gate into a field.

Follow the shallow depression of an old canal curving right. The bridleway forks left to a gate onto the Gloucester - Newent road. Instead, turn right on a footpath from the road, through a gate, and then over a stile on the left.

Begun in 1792 and completed in 1845, the Herefordshire and Gloucestershire canal was virtually forgotten until recent years. From the Severn at Gloucester via Newent, Dymock and Ledbury the canal was 34 miles in length with 22 locks and three tunnels. The canal closed in 1881 to allow the construction of the Gloucester to Newent railway and the track was laid along some lengths of the canal bed. The Three Choirs Way meets the canal again between Hereford and Worcester.

Follow the track bed of the old railway for about 300 yards to a stile on the left. Over this walk alongside the hedge for a similar distance to a lane at Rudford. Cross to a kissing gate and descend the embankment to regain the track bed and follow it for three quarters of a mile.

At a road, cross over and climb the grass embankment up to Barbers Bridge above the site of the Railway Station. From the bridge turn right along a headland path to Bovone Farm. From a gate the public path continues straight on between farm buildings and then forks diagonally left down to gate. *Barbarous Bridge - from a Civil War action.*

Walk left, around the hedge corner and cross the field to a footbridge. Continue behind houses to a road and turn right down to a junction. Turn right and then left, past the village duckpond, and walk up to a footpath along a track on the right, just prior to Tibberton church.

The track descends, *with May Hill and Ragged Stone Hill at the end of the Malverns prominent,* to open fields and a junction of paths. Fork left across a field to a stile, then inclining left, walk a long field to double stiles and continue to a footbridge into parkland. Again incline left, leaving oak trees to the right and cross a farm drive to a gate in the hedge ahead, just to the right of a concrete farm road.

From the gate depart from the Wysis Way, which continues straight ahead towards May Hill, instead fork right, climbing the shoulder of the slight ridge, on a line towards two tall conifers on the horizon, and then down to a gate. *The situation may be confused by the farmer providing paths through crops on slightly different lines to the correct routes.* Two paths diverge from the gate, the left leading to Taynton church, a pleasant spot to pause.

The original church was burnt down during the Civil War and replaced in 1650. It is unique, being aligned 'the wrong way'. The fir trees are Wellingtonia Sequoias, set between Limes. This ancient pastoral scene is completed by a Victorian post box set in the church yard wall.

From the church, in the absence of a stile opposite, turn right down the road, to a track on the left, to Drew's Farm. Cross a stream and follow the track until past the line of the farm buildings and turn left through a gate. Walk along the field edge to a stile. Continue across the next field through a gate into the farm yard at The Hill. Incline right past the farmhouse and along the farm drive, and where this bends left fork right into a green lane. *The surface needs care as large lumps of concrete rubble have been deposited across the full width with little thought for pedestrians or animals.*

Emerging into open field, the line of the old way can be traced along the boundary hedge to the next corner. Now change direction by climbing the stile and bank on the right, to *Cole's Barn.*

Walk directly down the large field, cross a stream and climb the slope keeping about 50 yards from the trees on the right, surrounding Ploddy House. From the brow continue straight down to join the Taynton - Newent road and turn right passing Little Cugley. Around a bend, under an oak tree, turn left on a footpath and walk, angling right, over a low ridge, to a stile. Over this incline left towards the hedge and, after a 150 yards go through a field gate and turn uphill to a stile.

Climb the stile, and another on the left, and descend the field alongside the hedge, accompanied by the dominating presence of electricity pylons and power lines, both local and national grid, to a further stile. Descend steps and cross the undulating field midway between the power lines. Close to the next boundary, incline left to a gate under the trees.

Through the gate the ground is sometimes boggy. Following the hedge on the right climb the short slope of an earth dam, where a lake has been created, and keep right around the edge of the pleasant stretch of water.

From the lake walk to the gate and continue along the track beyond, *passing a pen of peacocks on the left.* At a road, continue straight on, alongside Newent Wood, for half a mile rounding a right hand bend, with an old perry orchard over the hedge. *Cider was once a common drink in rural areas, every farm had a cider orchard and most cottages at least one apple or pear tree. Perry, as its name suggests, was made solely from pears.*

Continue over a narrow crossroad uphill, with cottages on the right, until the road surface reverts to a track. After the last cottage climb a stile on the right, and walk up the field aiming right of a red roofed cottage. *Leaving the field, lean on the gate for a moment and, trying to ignore the forest of pylons, take in the wide panorama over the vale. If the weather is reasonable, or even sunny, Gloucester cathedral will be clear in the distance.*

From the gate walk up the lane to a junction where the lane bends right and continue straight ahead over a stile alongside a gate. Walk past a horse training arena and gradually converge with the hedge on the right at a gate. *The view, improved by the lack of pylons, is now west and north to Mayhill and Herefordshire, with the Marcle ridge dominated by its tall mast. In the distance the Suckley hills beyond the long ridge of the Malverns.*

Walk down the field towards the hedge on the left and where this bends left, continue across the field to a stile in the cross hedge. Continue across the next field to emerge onto a track just left of a house, *Ravenshill*.

Go through the gate opposite and walk down the headland track past a gate on the right, for about 150 yards to an overgrown gate. Cross and continue down the other side of the hedge, *again with extensive views from this slight ridge,* to a stile at the bottom of the field.

Climb the slight slope of the field in front and walk down to the boundary of another house, *Briery Hill.* Pass the first gate into the property but, in another 20 yards, turn left through a second gate, and walk down the drive to exit through a further gate or a gap alongside.

Continue down the track, as it levels alongside woodland and just after a cottage branch left through trees to the Newent - Ross road. Cross to a narrow lane and follow this at Kilcot.

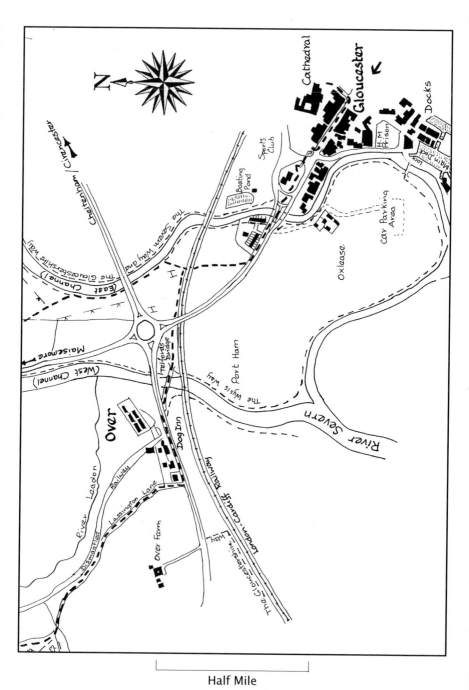

Half Mile

Reproduced by kind permission of Ordnance Survey © Crown Copyright MC/99-073

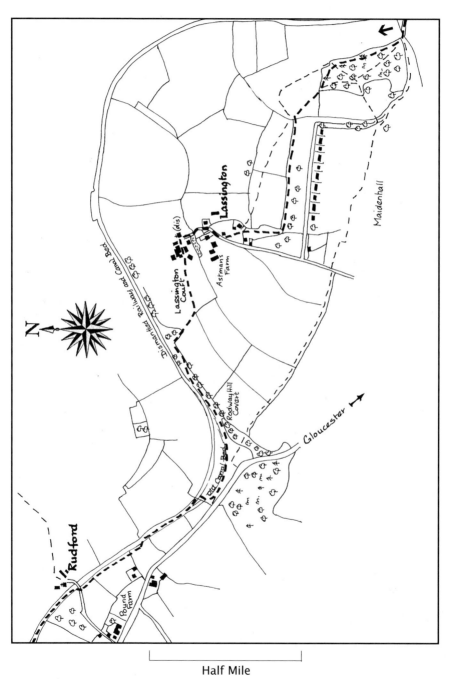

N

Lassington

Lassington

(dis)

Lassington Court

Astmans Farm

Maidenhall

Dismantled Railway and Canal Bed

Rodway Hill Covert

Gloucester

Old Canal Bed

Rudford

Pound Farm

Half Mile

Reproduced by kind permission of Ordnance Survey © Crown Copyright MC/99-073

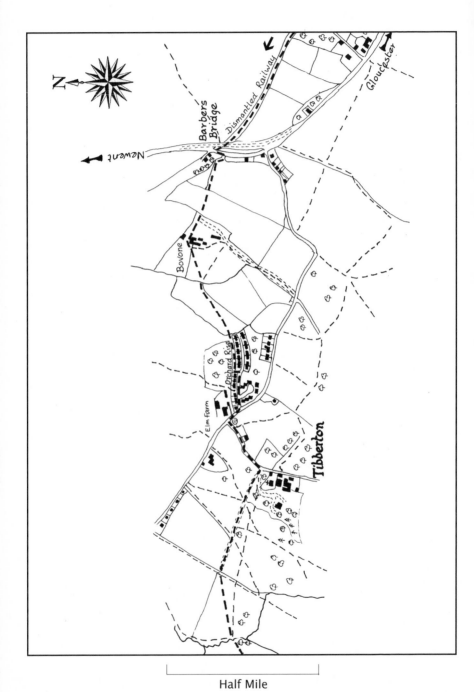

Half Mile

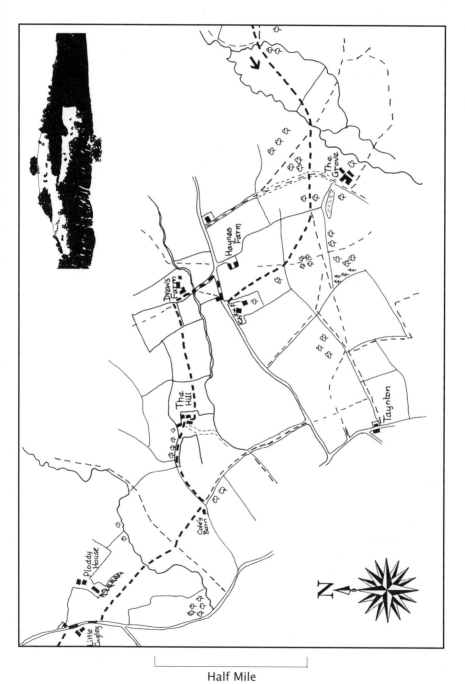

Half Mile

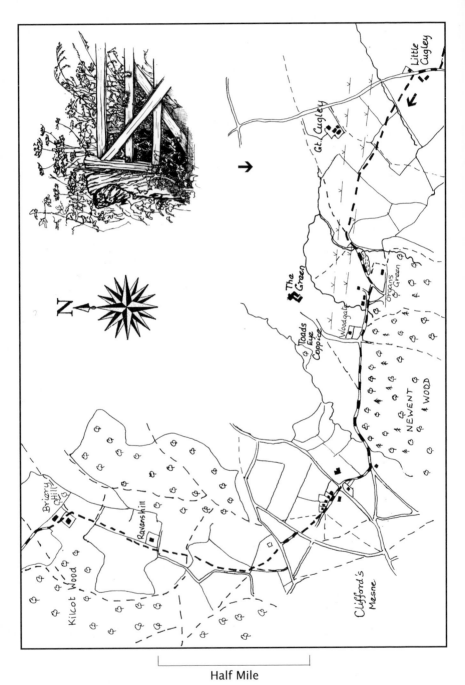

Little Cugley

Gt. Cugley

The Green

Organs Green

Woodgate

Toads Eye Coppice

NEWENT WOOD

Briery Hill

Ravenshill

Kilcot Wood

Clifford's Mesne

N

Half Mile

Reproduced by kind permission of Ordnance Survey © Crown Copyright MC/99-073

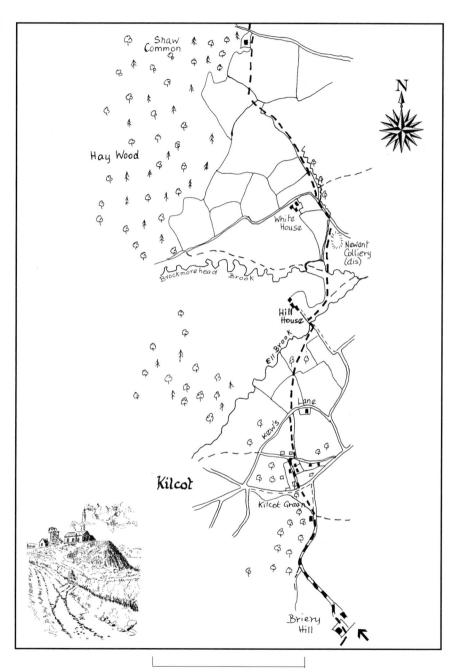

Shaw Common

Hay Wood

White House

Newant Colliery (dis)

Brockmorehead Brook

Hill House

Ell Brook

Lane

Kaw's

Kilcot

Kilcot Green

Briery Hill

Half Mile

Reproduced by kind permission of Ordnance Survey © Crown Copyright MC/99-073

Kilcot to Haugh Wood

At a junction turn right, past a creeper covered farmhouse and large barn, to a footpath on the left and walk down the field, alongside the hedge, to a gate onto Kews Lane. Turn right for a few paces and then left through a gate into a field and bear right down to an gate in the corner.

Continue, half right, down through an old cider orchard, past a hedge corner, to the Ell Brook. Around a bend climb a stile up to a track to Hill House Farm. Turn left, crossing the brook, and after 50 yards, right through a gate.

Nearby is the site of Hill House Colliery. Coal alleged to be plentiful hereabouts was a major persuasion for the funding of the Hereford-Gloucester Canal and the path follows the line of a mile long branch from Oxenhall.

Cross the field, keeping below the steep bank through a gap in an old boundary, and follow the hedge on the left for 100 yards until it bends away left. Now cross the low lying meadow to a hunt gate opposite, on an embankment. *This is actually a culvert of 1790, which carried the branch canal over Brockmorehead Brook, which the canal then followed towards Oxenhall.*

Through the gate keep left, following a lesser stream along a narrow valley to a gate onto a lane. *The steep hillocks on the right are the spoil heaps of Newent Colliery which once occupied the site.*

Turn left and after about 200 yards, join a footpath through a gate on the right. Walk up the meadow, ignoring a path on the right, to a stile and continue alongside the hedge towards a cottage on the horizon. Cross a stile and small plateau, *where a sudden view opens to the left, of Mayhill and the Forest of Dean hills,* to another stile, and then branch right to a further stile in an angle of the hedge. Walk up the next field towards the cottage and follow the garden boundary to a gate on to a road. *The cottage is tile hung in the style of the Sussex Weald.*

Turn left for twenty yards to a gate on the right and walk down to a pond and a kissing gate into Greenaways Wood. Keep left just inside the wood edge and descend to a narrow slab bridge over a stream. Walk directly up the opposite slope where Greenaways Cottage comes into view. The correct line passes to the right around the cottage and joins an access track to a road. A well used path may be found left of the cottage, which also join the track. Turn right, accompanied by the noise and rush of traffic on the invisible motorway.
We are complacent of this blight, but walking along this otherwise quiet lane through the woodland landscape of the Dymock Poets, it seems a great pity.

> . . . I had a song, too, on my road,
> But mine was in my eyes;
> For Malvern Hills were with me all the way,
> Singing loveliest visible melodies
> Blue as a south-sea bay;
> And ruddy as wine of France. . .
> veil'd in streamers of grey wavering smoke
> My shapely Malvern Hills. . .
>
> *Lascelles Abercrombie*

In the years leading up to the First World War, literary history was being made in the valley of the Leadon around Dymock. Although the 'muse colony' as they came to be known; Lascelles Abercrombie, Wilfred Gibson and Robert Frost; were not Gloucestershire poets, they received many visitors during their stay who were also destined to become well known. Of these, Rupert Brooke, perhaps the most well known, and Edward Thomas, were shortly to die in war. Among the local poets who visited the colony, John Drinkwater and WH Davies later lived in the county. John Haines, a Gloucester solicitor, was a regular visitor and particular friend of Robert Frost. Haines encouraged Ivor Gurney, a fellow choral scholar of Herbert Howells, and FW (Will) Harvey who were to become acknowledged poets of Gloucestershire.

Cross the motorway, and after 150 yards turn left onto a footpath through Dymock Wood. Part of the local Daffodil Way, the path may be waymarked.

The Daffodil Way is a circular route of ten miles, through an area which once provided seasonal work for itinerant Daffodil pickers, the city markets being supplied by rail. Although much diminished, the woods and hedgerows are still thick with wild varieties in the spring.

The track soon bends right over an open area, then curving left, take a right fork into slightly denser woodland. Follow the twists and turns of the track, with young oak woodland to the right, in Kempley Parish, and beech to the left, in Newent. *Sessile oak is prominent and typical of the border with Wales. Acorns are collected by Forest Enterprise and stored at a nursery at Delamere in Cheshire for distribution.*

Keep right at the next fork and shortly cross a stoned Forestry road. The path emerges from the wood over a stile into the remains of a cider orchard.

Cross a brook near a willow tree and walk up towards farm buildings. Go through the left of two adjacent farm gates and along the line of an old track, bounded on the left by a row of old Perry trees and on the right by wide views to the Malvern ridge. Continue past the barns and a knot of trees, *Poplar, oak and two pear trees,* to a stile in the corner, and walk up the headland beneath *Turkey oaks.*

Over another stile, then walk between gardens into Kempley Green *passing a Chapel (1856).* Within a few yards the Daffodil Way turns left, but continue for another 200 yards and fork right into a green lane, not to be confused with a footpath to the right. *Footpath signposts left and right of the road are sometimes hidden by overhanging shrubbery.* Continue along the green lane, crossing a farm track, through a gate and then along a field edge. *Ahead, in the middle distance is the church tower of Much Marcle, with Marcle ridge, and ubiquitous mast, further left.* Just before the next boundary, go through a gate on the left and turn right down to a stile.

Kempley has two churches. St Edwards, built in 1903, can be visited by a footpath to the left climbing the field. It has several modern sculptures and was described by John Betjeman as 'a minature cathedral of the Arts and Crafts movement'.

Continue alongside the hedge, slightly uphill and curving right, to a gate onto a lane. Turn left and walk down for a 100 yards, to a footpath on the right under the branches of a large oak. Follow the hedge of this long field, with a stream on the other side, to a gate just before Kempley Court. Bear right following the stream, passing a footbridge on the right and leaving the farm buildings to the left, towards the squat tower of Kempley Church. Cross a footbridge and then a large stone slab, over tributaries of Kempley Brook, to St Mary's church. *Containing extensive frescoes, some of which are as fresh as when painted in 1130, the building is now managed by English Heritage.*

31

At the road turn left, and cross to a gate and angle right across the corner of the field to a stile. Keep left close to the ditch line for about 60 yards, and then bear right to a stile in the hedge. Angle right to converge with the next hedgerow, and after about 100 yards cross a stile and plank bridge.

Turn left to a further stile and footbridge, then cross a narrow field below *Friar's Court,* followed by a long field to a stile and then a short field to a footbridge in a thick hedge, *the boundary between Gloucestershire into Herefordshire.* Cross two more fields to reach the road from Dymock, and turn left into Much Marcle which has a village shop and three pubs. *Mear- cleah,* o*ld English - a boundary wood.*

Enter the churchyard through a yew lychgate and pass an ancient cross to the famed and impressive Marcle Yew. *Thought to be at least 1500 years old, stand beside it and consider the history which the tree stood silent witness to since Roman times.*

Nearby the 'Wonder Landslide' of 1575 must have been impressive, not only because a huge amount of hillside moved several hundred yards, but because it did so slowly during three days. They must have thought it the end of the world.

Unlettered carpenters,
After four hundred years
Nothing is left of them,
Even their bones are dust.

They put the axe to oak,
The saw, adze and chisel;
Unlettered carpenters
Nothing is left of them

Whose eyes grew narrower
From saw-pit to grave-pit;
After four hundred years
Even their bones are dust.

Unlettered carpenters,
After four hundred years,
All that is left of them -
V V O O X X
Geoffrey Mason
(Carpenters marks on local cottages)

Leave the churchyard under another yew arch and cross a track to a stile. Descend the field, diagonally right to the corner and a hidden gate. Cross a road to a similar gate and from this angle slightly left across the field to a footbridge.

Continue on the same line up to a stile and follow the headland of a long field up to a minor road. Slightly left, climb a stile and walk up the slope, inclining right over the shoulder of the ridge to another minor road. Cross this into an enclosed track and follow this winding uphill past cottages at Marcle Hill. *There are splendid views behind and to the north from these slopes. Ledbury is clearly seen below the Malvern ridge, and beyond Marcle Church, the Severn plain to the Cotswold scarp.*

John Masefield was born at Ledbury in 1878, and the countryside around the Malvern Hills and Hereford influenced his works throughout his life. His vigorous narrative poems, like 'The Everlasting Mercy', and 'Reynard the Fox', and less known lyrics and sonnets are colourful descriptions of the local countryside. Fittingly, for a time, he and Elgar were the country's pre-eminent poet and musician, he as Poet Laureate and Elgar as Master of the King's Music.

Cross a stile at Marcle Hill cottage and turn left to a further stile, over this turn right and follow the hedge bending left to join a track at *Little Puckmore*. Walk up to a lane and turn uphill for 300 yards to a sharp bend. *Pause, leaning on a handy field gate, to sample the views again. From this increased elevation all the outlying hills of Cotswold can be identified, and in the south Mayhill seems close at hand. Under a westering sun Gloucester Cathedral stands clearly in the vale.*

Leave the lane and continue uphill on a rough track. As this starts to descend sharply, turn right climbing a stile and steps up to the Marcle ridge. *Before doing so it is worth stepping left to a field gate for the changed vista over the ridges and woods of the Forest of Dean and the far flung hills of Wales.* Climb the ridge for a few yards and cross a stile on the left, and then walk up the enclosed track for three quarters of a mile, passing the mast and then a Trig point. *Through occasional gaps in the trees the Black Mountains, from Skirrid and the Sugar Loaf up to Hay Bluff unfolds under a vast panorama of mid Wales.*

Shortly after the Trig point the track becomes a headland path where the westerly views are curtailed by Hoar Wood. After a further half mile the path joins a road at *Sleaves Oak, a small picnic area maintained by Herefordshire Countryside Service.*

Walk down the narrow lane descending to the left, for a quarter of a mile, passing the house *Sleaves Oak.* The lane bends right and then sharply left. Turn right through a gate under trees, and zig zag down the contours. Pass a barn and turn left along a farm track to Hyde Farm. Ignore a gate and stile straight on at the farm yard, but follow the track right between farm buildings, where it shortly becomes a public road.

In less than half a mile after a left bend and where the road begins to descend, cross a stile, alongside a gate, on the right and walk down a field past a clump of young *Horse Chestnuts, Oaks and Limes.* Cross a footbridge and walk half right across an apple orchard to a stile and immediately left to a further stile. Over this, continue diagonally up to a hedge corner, *where the squat tower of Woolhope Church appears on the skyline.* Continue on a line to the right of houses, and cross two stiles to a road.

Commencing long before the Roman occupation Herefordshire has a long history of cider making, where mild springs and warm summers promote tree growth and ripen the fruit.
Thomas Knight of Hereford, was the first systematic cultivator of new apple varieties. His 'Pomona Herefordiensis' of 1691, was the first illustrated book describing cider apples and pears. The original cider apple was small and bitter, but some 265 varieties evolved through the art of grafting and budding.
Cider orchards which once enhanced many farms have gone. Today's cider is, in the main, commercially produced from limited varieties to maintain a standard product far removed from traditional cider.

'Coccagee and Bloody Butcher:
Slack- ma-Girdle,
Red Soldier and Lady's Finger,
Kingston Black, Bloody Turk,
Foxwhelp, Pawson, Tom Putt,
Bitter Sweet and Fatty Mutt.'

Turn left and walk up to the Crown Inn and, possibly, welcome refreshment. An old paved path leads into the adjoining churchyard beneath two grand Lime trees.

A long way from Coventry, a window in the church features Lady Godiva - properly Godgifu, she and her sister Wuliva are connected with Woolhope because they once owned the manor. Woolhope may be contracted from 'Wuliva's Hope', -Hope being an enclosed valley or hollow.

The 'Woolhope Dome' is an interesting geological area of rocks and fossils and a particular limestone. Woolhope spawned a Naturalists Field Club in 1854 an early president bring Alfred Watkins of Hereford, who propounded the theory of Ley Lines, not yet proved entirely wrong.

Pass the church, go through a gate into the carpark and turn left to the road. Turn right and cross over to a kissing gate into a field. Walk close to an oak tree and follow the edge of woodland to the right. Continue through a second kissing gate and, after 50 yards, a third, into the woodland. Follow a stream bed uphill to an obvious crossing, where the stream has been dammed, and turn right, through pleasant meadow land. *Marked 'The Leys' on the OS map - medieval pasture or fallow land.*

After a final kissing gate, walk uphill to a gate onto a road and turn right, soon passing alongside part of Broadmoor Common. Continue past a road junction and houses at Haugh Wood Gate.

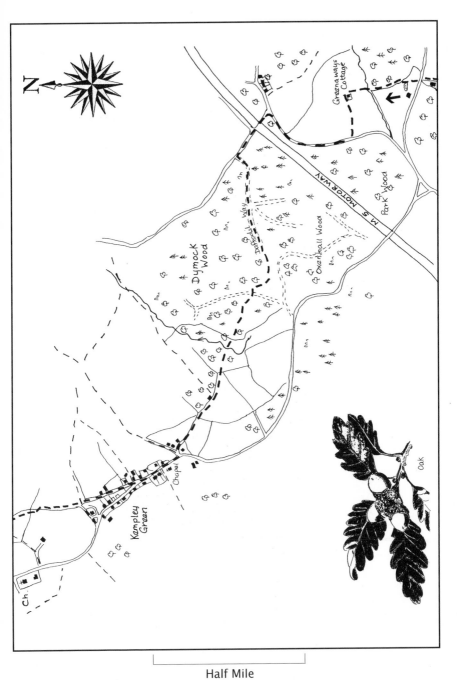

N

Greenaways Cottage

M S MOTOR WAY

Park Wood

Dymock Wood

Dutch Way

Oxanhall Wood

Chapel

Kempley Green

Ch.

Oak

Half Mile

Reproduced by kind permission of Ordnance Survey © Crown Copyright MC/99-073

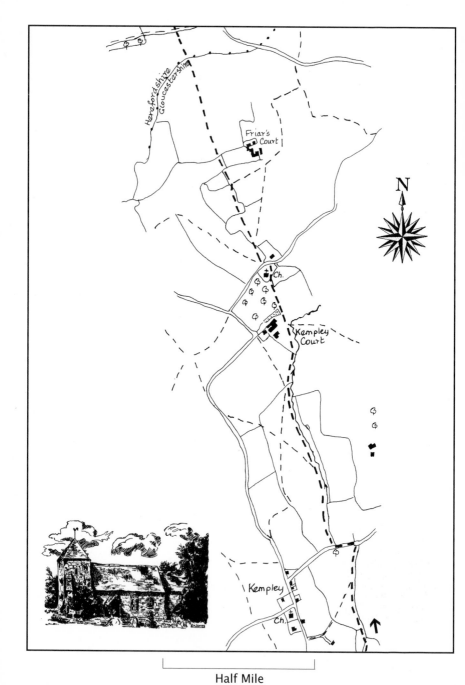

Half Mile

Reproduced by kind permission of Ordnance Survey © Crown Copyright MC/99-073

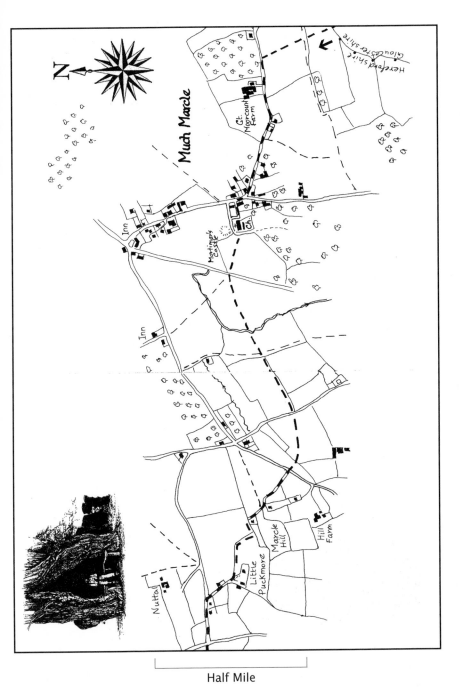

Half Mile

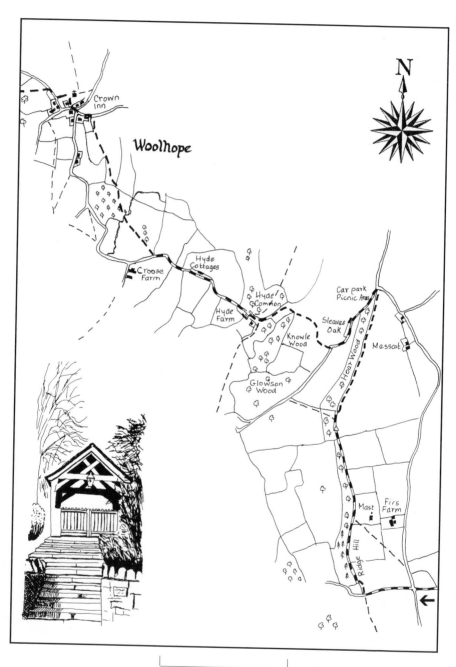

N

Crown Inn

Woolhope

Croose Farm

Hyde Cottages

Hyde Common

Hyde Farm

Car park Picnic Area

Sleaves Oak

Knowle Wood

Hoar Wood

Masscot

Glowson Wood

Mast

Firs Farm

Ridge Hill

Half Mile

Reproduced by kind permission of Ordnance Survey © Crown Copyright MC/99-073

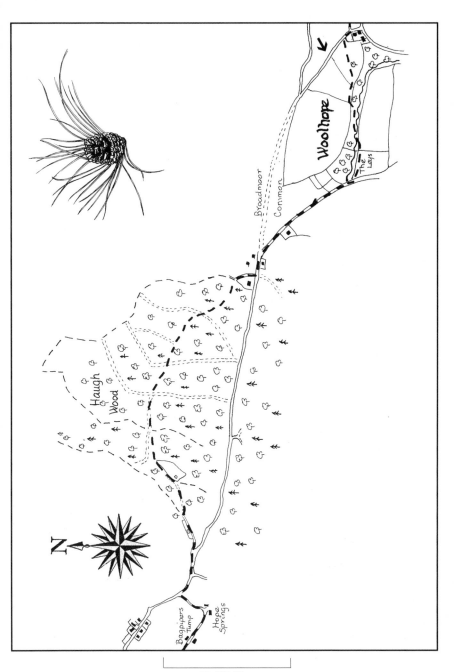

Woolhope

Broadnaor Common

Haugh Wood

The Leys

Bagpipers Tump

Hope Springs

N

Half Mile

Haugh Wood to Withington

After a red brick cottage, turn right onto a bridleway, but in a few yards, at a vehicle barrier, branch left onto a footpath. Ignore a left fork and continue on the main path, often wet in places, rising steadily through Haugh Wood, - *old English, haga - an enclosure, in this case of trees.* '*A man- eating dragon once resided here, using a path, still called Serpent's Lane, down to Mordiford to terrorise the locality*'.

The path levels and then descends over a major cross path before climbing again to join a forestry road at a bend. Follow this to the right, ignoring a lesser track branching right, and descend to cross another forestry road.

At the next cross path turn left and then immediately right, descending into an old hollow way. The entrance can be overlooked, particularly if the waymark post is overgrown. *Throughout Europe, new forestry roads, particularly in hill areas, are created with little sympathy or attempt to preserve the original paths and tracks, often of great antiquity.*
Walk down this old route beneath a grove of cedars and emerge near a small paddock. Pass a gate and turn left along the edge of woodland, to a stile. Join a track, passing a cottage, and continue pleasantly down for

a quarter of a mile, to the Woolhope - Mordiford road.

Turn right for about 300 yards, and then left on a bridleway which descends curving left, to Hope Springs. Nearing the buildings go through a gate and turn right into an enclosed track, *now shared with the Wye Valley Walk,* up past houses at *Bagpiper's Tump.*

> *The Wye Valley Walk commences at Chepstow Castle and follows, for 70 miles, the beautiful Wye Valley to Tintern, and then the meandering river past Monmouth, Ross-on Wye and Hereford, to Hay-on-Wye, deep in the Welsh Marches.*

Where the bridleway jinks left between buildings, find a footpath on the right, sometimes obscured by undergrowth, descending through a green tunnel. Continue over a stile and down through a pleasant orchard following the hedge on the left. Cross a stream and follow this, crossing again at a farm bridge, then keep right of farm buildings to a gate into the farm yard. Walk down to a road at Mordiford, -*Welsh, mawr-ty - a great house.* Either cross and follow a back lane to Mordiford Bridge and Church, or turn right to detour past the Moon Inn, Ye Olde Shoppe and Post Office in the village centre.

The village grew around an ancient ford over the River Lugg. The original bridge dates from the 14th Century but was enlarged in the 16th. Two arches take the normal flow but all nine are necessary in time of flood.

The church records an occurrence. . . 'on Monday, 27th May, 1811, between the hours of 5 and 9pm the village of Mordiford was visited by a terrible storm, thunder, lightning, winds and rain, by which the little river of Pentaloe was swollen in places to extent of 180 feet and depth of 20 feet'. . . Four villagers were drowned.

Cross the bridge and flood arches, and turn right onto a footpath along the floodbank *(the Stank)*, and follow this alongside the Lugg for more than a mile to Hampton Bishop. A public path crosses the fields more directly but the riverside route is not so susceptible to floodwater and provides wider views.

Go through a gate, joining a track from the village, and through a second gate follow the track to a barn. Leave the track and cross a field to a metal gate and stile. Continue along the edge of an orchard to a gate onto a lane to Court Farm. Turn left, ignoring another lane to the right, to a road, and follow this to the right between houses. Shortly, be alert for a footpath on the right, where the signpost and access are set back under trees.

The path follows the edge of a field, and continues across another field to a stile onto a lay-by alongside the Mordiford to Hereford road. *From the lay-by buses are available into Hereford. The 'Bunch of Carrots' Inn is 100 yards left.*

Cross to the wider verge and turn right for 20 yards. Climb the flood bank and turn right, through a kissing gate and along the flood bank, to a second kissing gate. Leave the floodbank, *with the Wye Valley Walk,* and over a footbridge cross the field diagonally, to the bank of the River Wye.

Follow the riverside path through water meadows and kissing gates. The spire of Tupsley Church, above pink roofs ahead, shows the line of the Three Choirs out of Hereford towards Worcester. Near a large oak tree, incline right to a final gate, and a gravelled path between new houses, to the road.

Alternative Route

Walkers who may not wish to visit the City, or prefer to avoid four miles of roads involved, can follow a shortcut more directly to Lugwardine. Turn right for 200 yards to a bridleway on the left, and follow Holywell Gutter Lane for almost a mile to a road near

Tupsley School. Turn right to Ledbury Road, alongside the 'Cock of Tupsley'. Should you visit this hostelry, remember on leaving either to cross to the lane opposite or to turn right.

No common waters, by these ancient walls,
Flow from Plynlimon's distant storm-filled springs,
By many a changing mile the current brings
By Ithon's vale and Ebbw's rock-bound falls
And mountain moorlands where the curlew calls
A spell distilled of old and lovely things;
Cloud wrapped memorials of long dead Kings,
Forsaken castles and deserted halls.
The scattered dust of centuries lies blown
Along the valleys where the oaks are green,
Dressed by the summers of a thousand years
And all the sun and rain the years have known,
For all that is born of what has been;
From age to age its laughter and its tears.

Robert Wade

Otherwise turn left towards Hereford. After about a mile, pass under a railway bridge and turn immediately left into *Outfall Works Road*. Walk down this narrow road for about 400 yards, and just before crossing a small viaduct turn right down the embankment to a footpath crossing fields to Green Street.

The name invokes an image of the medieval approach to the city walls close about the Cathedral and Castle mound, and the relief felt by travellers after the tales of dragons in Haugh Wood and fear of floodwaters at Mordiford.

Walk along Green Street for 50 yards and turn left into Vicarage Road. Pass a school and continue down a footpath to the river bank and turn right to the *Victoria* footbridge. Do not cross, but climb the steps to

Castle Green, *(site of Hereford Castle)* and cross to the narrow streets around the cathedral.

Anglo Saxon Charters refer to Here-paths, - literally meaning Army roads. Hereford may well have taken its name from a ford across the Wye 'the army ford' where Roman armies crossed in safety and the only method until a wooden bridge was built in the 12th Century. When that was destroyed by flood waters Richard II provided materials for repairs and granted toll rights for twenty years. The present Wye Bridge was built in 1490.

Established as a cathedral city in 676 AD, a stone cathedral existing before the Conquest was destroyed by Welsh invaders in 1055. The present building was begun by the Normans soon after their arrival. The cathedral contains two unique treasures. The Mappa Mundi is a 13th Century map or 'estoire' - a history, on vellum. The coloured map, shows the world as a circle with Jerusalem at the centre and 'Britainnia Insula' almost off the edge, and contains a wealth of detail with the 'Wie' and 'Hford' marked.

The 'chained library', the largest in England, contains 1500 priceless books and manuscripts from as early as 1056 although the bookcases, with each volume chained to a horizontal bar, was introduced in 1611. Hereford also boasts the second largest 'chained library', in All Saints Church.

David Garrick was born in Hereford in 1717 and Nell Gwynne, actress and favourite mistress of Charles II, is said to have been born here in 1651.

Sir Edward Elgar rose from obscurity to become England's greatest composer for 200 years. His connection with Hereford began when he was playing his violin with both the Choral and Philharmonic Societies in the early 1880's, and he must have taken part in many Musical Festivals. After marrying, he lived at Great Malvern from 1891 until 1904, during which he was a regular visitor to Dr George

Robertson Sinclair, organist at Hereford. Elgar dedicated various works to Dr Sinclair, who with his dog Dan, is celebrated in the 'Enigma Variations' arising from an occasion when Dan slid down the steep river bank into the Wye. After receiving his knighthood in 1904 Elgar moved to Hereford where he composed some his best works, including the Violin Concerto and his two Symphonies. Elgar had a great love of the countryside and of the Wye which is reflected in his great choral music. Parts of 'The Musicmakers' are said to have been composed at Mordiford Bridge.

From the cathedral retrace your steps to Castle Street and continue into St Ethelbert Street. After passing Cantilope Street, turn right along St Owen's Street and after a short distance left into Bath Street. Cross the road to a footpath just left of Daw's Road and walk down this and then the length of Central Avenue. Towards the bottom cross to the elevated pavement and follow this curving round to join the Ledbury Road. This can be followed directly to Lugwardine, but a slight variation is preferable.

After a roundabout, continue for 300 yards and turn right into Quarry Road. Pass Dormington Drive on the left and then turn into a path beneath trees and shrubs adjacent to Tupsley Park. When this ends, turn right into Church Road and immediately left into Winchester Drive, merging into Salisbury Avenue and leads to Ledbury Road again.

Walk along the major road for about 350 yards and, opposite 'The Cock of Tupsley', (where the alternative route avoiding Hereford re-joins) follow another quiet variation left, to Lower House Farm. *The headquarters of Herefordshire Nature Trust, the old farmhouse is well worth a visit.*

Continuing, rejoin the Ledbury Road and cross Tupsley Bridge followed by the causeway across the flood meadows, and finally Lugwardine Bridge, *where an iron plaque informs passersby that the cost of widening the bridge was met by 'local neighbourhood subscription and at the expense of the County'. A few yards further on pass an unusual cast iron trough and working pump.*

After 400 yards turn left into Cott Road at Lugwardine, where the Crown and Anchor Inn may provide the first refreshment after Hereford.

> *Lugwardine - settlement by the Lugg.*
> *The water meadows cover several hundreds of acres and are part of a system of Tenure which has survived from pre-medieval times. Known as Lammas Lands, they are grazed 'in common', when the animals wander freely, from Lammas, 2nd August, to Candlemas, 2nd February. For the remainder of the year hay is grown 'in severalty', with individual strips separated from neighbouring strips by boundary stones. Problems and disputes are settled at an annual meeting at the Crown and Anchor Inn.*

Past the pub follow the bend and after the last bungalow join a footpath on the right. Follow the field edge, but after the first boundary hedge veer left to a stile. The path divides beyond the stile and either can be taken. The left fork continues through a hand gate, over a stream and inclines right to join a stony track in front of a white thatched cottage. Follow this up to a road and turn right.

After 100 yards, with the road bending right, turn left on a footpath sometimes hidden in shrubbery alongside a bungalow. The path is narrow at first, but at a stile join a track uphill, through another gate alongside a pond. At the next field boundary continue across an open field to a further boundary, but here turn left without crossing.

> *The boundary is slightly elevated above the adjacent fields giving a wide panorama over north Herefordshire, with nearby Shucknall Hill to the right. The more spectacular view is behind. Above the squat tower of Lugwardine church are the Sugar Loaf and Skirrid. Beyond the cathedral is the long dark ridge of the Black mountains terminating at Hay Bluff, and merging into a background of Welsh hills.*

At the field corner jink right and left and follow a hedge down, with a view over the village of Withington and its slender spire which catches the eye for miles around. Cross a stile, with the hedge now on the right, and walk down the small field to the road at Hynett Moor. Turn left for a few paces to a path on the right into the yard of Hynett Farm, where the dogs may be noisy. Do not be intimidated by the enclosed yard, but walk slightly left under the lean-to roof, to a door with an old fashioned snicket latch -*put your finger in the hole and lift..*

Cross a lawn, then follow the hedge down to an open field and continue to a footbridge at the point where power lines converge with the stream. Cross the bridge, railway tracks and a field, to a handgate into a garden and walk through to a road. *The right of way has been encroached by fencing resulting in a narrow pinched path against the hedge.*

Turn right and after 300 yards, near a red brick building, cross to a foot path. Climb the slope of the field on a line to the right of a red brick house ahead and join a rough track for a few yards. Where this bends sharply left turn right through a gap in the hedge into a field. Climb the field diagonally right, to an angle of the hedge and follow this to emerge onto a track. Cross, slightly left, and walk down the field edge. At the bottom turn right into the adjoining field and descend steps into Withington.

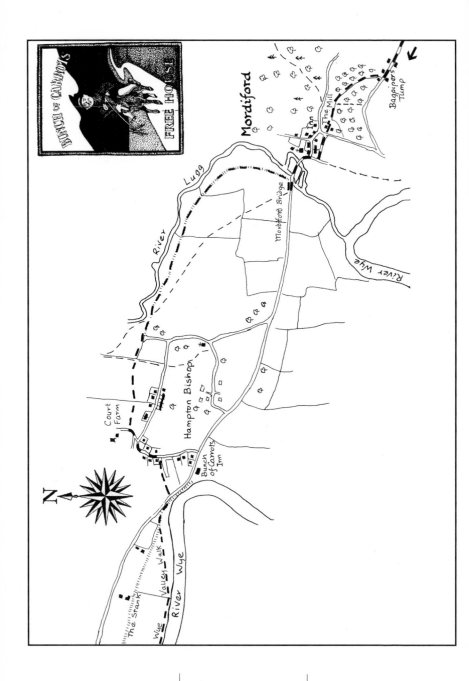

Half Mile

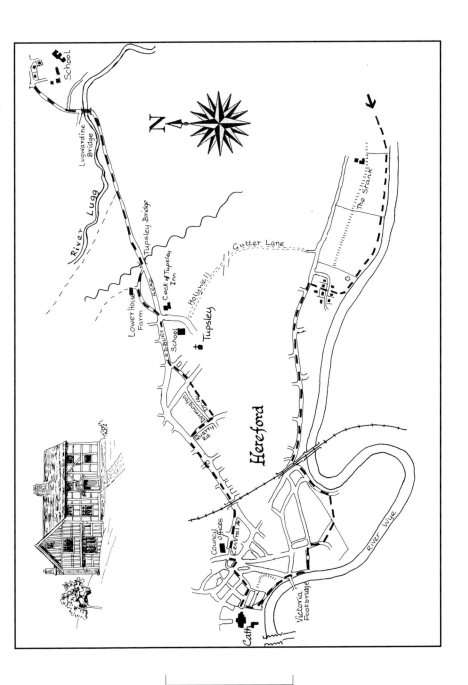

Half Mile

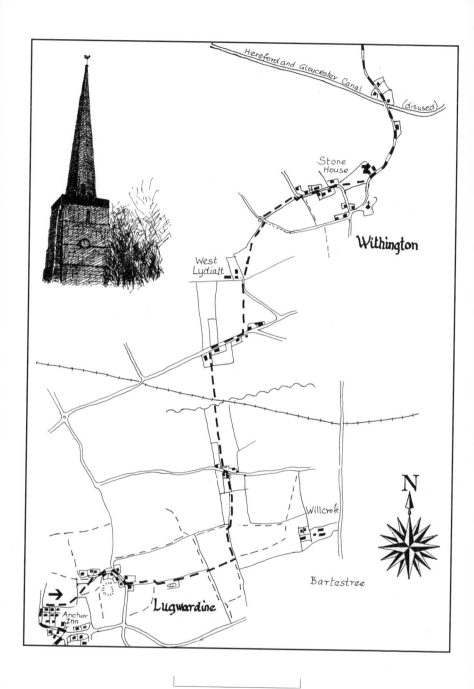

Half Mile

Withington to Stanford Bishop

Walk along the village street for 200 yards to a bend and continue straight on, through a gate, on a track inclining away from the farm buildings at *Stone House,* to a road. Turn left and follow the road for almost a mile, through a low lying area of Withington Marsh. *Withington - homestead among willows!*

Cross a stream and then the bed of the *old Hereford and Gloucester canal, last seen at Rudford.* For the next quarter mile the hedge bank is made pleasant, in spring and summer, by varieties of old fashioned roses planted beneath silver birch and acacia trees. Shortly, pass the sandstone buildings of Lower House Farm and turn right on a bridle-way at strangely named, Thing Hill Court *(Thigill locally)*

Past the farm buildings walk down to an isolated barn and follow the bridleway left. At a gate into open fields turn right along a short green lane, and then continue along the edge of three fields to Old Monkton Farm. Through a gate onto the farm track the bridleway turns left. A public footpath branching right from the bridleway has been encroached by farm buildings. Instead cross the track and past a building turn right to a field gate and through this turn left and resume on the right of way along the field edge.

Cross a stile in the corner and continue along the next headland to a stile and footbridge. From the bridge the public path forks right to Howberry Barn, from where another path, in the same field, crosses to a gate opposite the footbridge. Through the gate follow the field edge, to a further gate and then a long narrowing field rising to a stile in the furthest corner. Cross to a gate and walk along a short enclosed track to a road at Upper Castleton.

Turn left and follow a sharp bend beneath large oak trees, and at the next bend join a footpath angling up the field to emerge into a green lane and the village green at Ocle Pychard.

In old English, ac-leah - a grove or clearing in woodland. Recorded at Domesday as Acle. Roger Pichard, held the Manor in 1242, his name derives from pychard - old French for green woodpecker.
The 13th Century church has a copper covered spire and three mediaeval bells, the earliest cast in Worcester in 1410.

From the green turn right, *passing a Victorian post box*, and walk along the road for about three quarters of a mile, with wide views of rural Herefordshire, to the Ledbury - Leominster road.

Turn right for 50 yards and cross to a bridleway along a track to Cowarne Court. As the track descends slightly, the Malvern ridge shows above trees in front. At the farm complex turn left at the first opportunity, following a concrete road, left and then right, behind the buildings *which appear to have been built over the right of way.*

Fork left down a track and continue across a field along the line of the old headland to the end of the remaining hedge. The path forks left towards the church tower and a stile in the next hedge. Cross a low lying area and a footbridge, then fork left up to a stile into the churchyard at Much Cowarne, *old English - Cu-aern, a cowhouse.*

Walk, *beneath juniper and yews,* past the 14th century church and a gate to the car park, to a kissing gate. Turn right and walk down the church drive to a road junction. *Access to an adjacent footpath is discouraged by wired up gates.* Continue straight over for about 400 yards, to a footpath through a gate on the left. The footpath signpost may be slightly misaligned, but the public path follows the old field boundary, indicated by the trees ahead. After about 100 yards, fork right following the tree line down to cross the River Lodon.

Through a gate walk straight on, despite possibly confusing waymarks. From the next gateway follow the headland to a stile, and continue alongside the hedge with small ponds on the other side. Past the first pond fork away to a gate, hidden by the contour, in the cross hedge. *The public path from the gate to Hopes Rough Farm appears to have been stopped up by the erection of farm buildings.* Instead cross to the left of the red brick farmhouse where a waymark post indicates a route down to a gate onto the farm access track.

Walk up to a lane and turn left around a sharp bend, where a footpath joins from the left, and continue up to a road. *There is a dearth of footpaths in the vicinity. A route over Purley Hill ahead, would have been helpful. The quiet lanes must serve instead.*

Turn left for about 350 yards and then right into a lane, signposted Stoke Lacy, and follow this for three quarters of a mile. After several bends turn right on a footpath alongside a red bricked house, *Hopton Villa,* and follow a track uphill, past the dilapidated surroundings of Hopton Court. *As the track levels the higher ground obscures the view east, but a panorama opens left, extending to the shapely hills in the northwest, beyond Leominster, including Croft Ambury.*

Cross a stile next to a gate, and continue alongside the hedge for 200 yards into a short enclosed track. Near a house, cross to a gateway into a field. After a few yards angle uphill to re-join the track by a stile found about 40 yards before a cross hedge. Continue to the junction with *Stoke Lane* and follow this right for three quarters of a mile, passing a footpath on the left at *Richley Farm*. At *The Firs*, turn left through a gate and cross the corner of a field to a stile. Over this follow the hedge down the next field to a stile beneath willow trees and continue alongside the hedge, *with extensive views over pastoral Herefordshire.*

At the next hedge a gate leads into a green lane which emerges into the farmyard at Munderfield Court. Walk along the surfaced farm drive to a road at Munderfield Row. *Munderfield, originally Mundell's Feld - a large cleared area of Forest.*

From the stile opposite, cross the field slightly left and walk down the hedge to a stile in a hollow. Over this walk up the slope, again slightly left, to the ridge top. Turn left down this broad viewpoint to a stile and continue down the ridge to a stile alongside a gate in the angle of the next boundary. Follow the field edge beyond, over another stile alongside a gate, and continue alongside the fence curving down the undulating contours to Upper Venn farm. Walk to the right of a barn and join the farm track down to cross the River Frome, and then up to a road.

Turn left for 40 yards to a gate on the right where the path inclines right, away from the farm track, up a small valley to a stile in the hedge. Climb the slope slightly left, up to a wire fence and over this continue following the slight line of a track to a gate into a small enclosure and exit through a gate in the right hand corner. Continue uphill to a farm, *The Hawkins*. Go through a fieldgate and continue between farm buildings along the drive to the road at Stanford Bishop, *stoney ford, - the Manor was held by the Bishop of Hereford.*

The church stands in isolation among a few trees on a slight rise just south of The Hawkins. It contains a medieval chair which has excited historians in the past, in the belief that it may have been used by St Augustin in 603 AD !

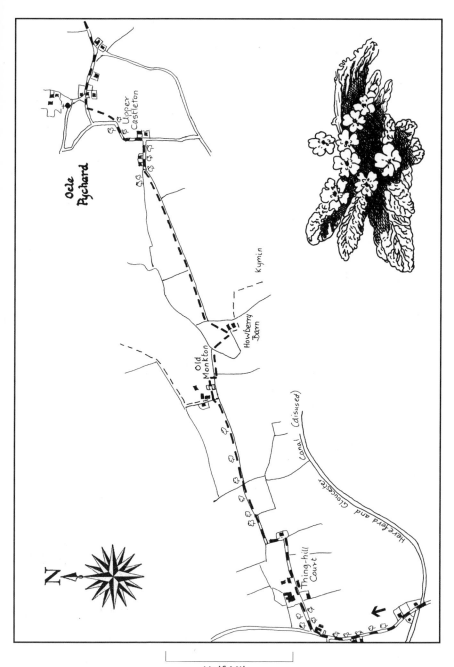

Ocle Pychard

Upper Castleton

Kymin

Howberry Barn

Old Monkton

Canal (disused)

Hereford and Gloucester

Thing-hill Court

N

Half Mile

Reproduced by kind permission of Ordnance Survey © Crown Copyright MC/99-

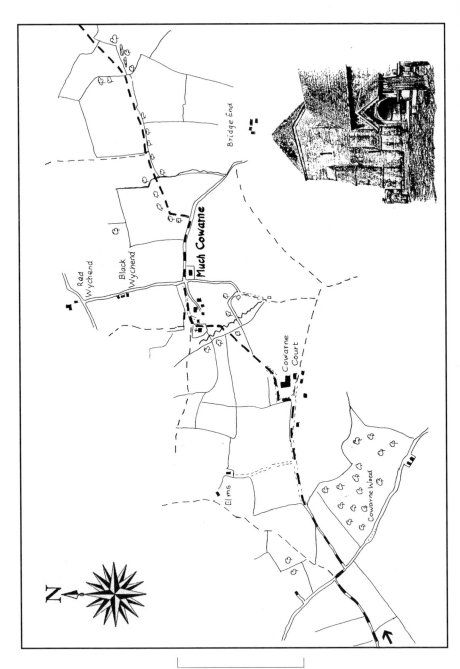

Bridge End

Much Cowarne

Red Wychend

Black Wychend

Cowarne Court

Elms

Cowarne Wood

N

Half Mile

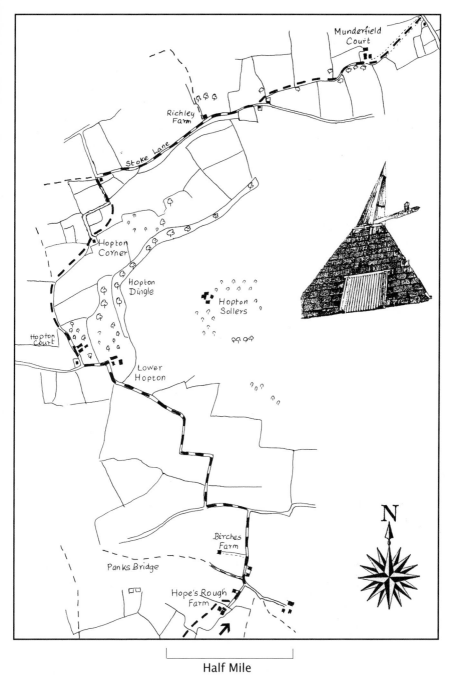

Munderfield Court

Richley Farm

Stoke Lane

Hopton Corner

Hopton Dingle

Hopton Sollers

Hopton Court

Lower Hopton

Birches Farm

Panks Bridge

Hope's Rough Farm

N

Half Mile

Reproduced by kind permission of Ordnance Survey © Crown Copyright MC/99-

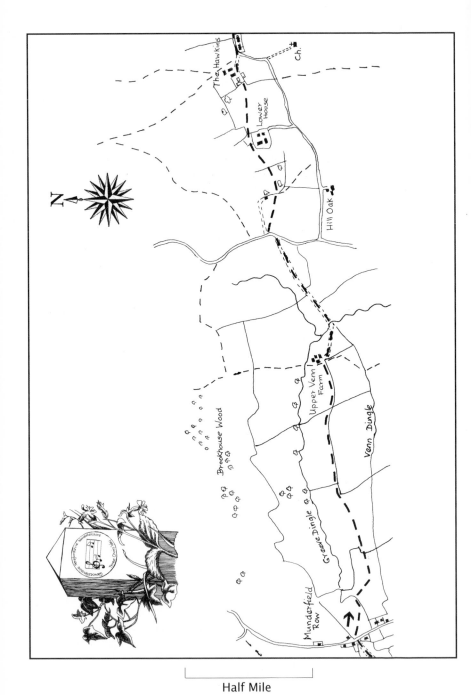

Half Mile

Stanford Bishop to Broadheath

Turn left along the road for half a mile to the Bromyard- Malvern road. The rest of the village, including a shop and pub, are off to the left. Turn right, and after about 200 yards, just past a cottage turn left into a track which soon becomes a headland path. Walk down the field edge to a stile into another enclosed section and emerge at a road.

Turn left for about 200 yards to a track on the right, just before a cottage. After 50 yards leave the track by a stile step in a new fence and continue with the hedge on the left. Cross two more stiles and then walk alongside a fence overlooking two small lakes. At a further stile fork left through young trees to a plank bridge and follow a hedge down to a footbridge. Walk up the next field, turn right through a gate and follow the hedge down to plank bridge over a stream. Cross this to a stile and walk up hill alongside the wood. After a 100 yards, at a cross path, turn left and continue up through the wood, over a stile, and under oak trees to a stile at the wood edge. *Cross this into Worcestershire.*

Turn left skirting the edge of the field and follow a thick hedge downhill. After about 200 yards the path switches to the other side of the hedge *(into Herefordshire again).* In another 200 yards cross a track to *Old*

Yearsett, and continue pleasantly alongside a stream.

Cross the stream and walk uphill to a gate at Upper House. Turn left, following a track, through a gate and close to the next gateway turn right over a stile. Walk up the field edge for 50 yards to a stile into a field on the left.

An electric fence inside the field has insulated handles to facilitate crossing. Walk up the field alongside the hedge on the right, through a gate, to Knowl Farm. Cross the yard, and through a gate, emerge onto to a road, alongside the Cross Keys Inn.

Cross to a stile opposite and angle left down the field to a headland track alongside an orchard. At a field gate continue across to the corner of the field and cross a rudimentary stile. Walk down the hedge for about 50 yards to a stile and cross the next field diagonally left to a stile at Suckley Row.

The three counties were well known for their apples, and for many the Worcester Pearmain, with its red streaked and juicy flesh, immediately comes to mind.

Six thousand varieties once grew in Britain and as recently as 1957 there were 64000 acres of dessert apples in England, now reduced to less than 25000 acres.

There has recently been a small resurgence of interest in the traditional apples with grants available in some areas to encourage the planting of old varieties.

'Apple Fairs' are increasingly popular autumn events, particularly in Herefordshire. Fortunately the National Fruit Trials Centre, where the worlds most comprehensive collection of apple varieties is preserved, exists in Kent.

Turn left and walk down the road, crossing the disused railway, and turn right signposted *Highfields*. In the absence of a stile on the left after 250 yards, continue, and just prior to the railway again turn left through a gate and cross a field to the remains of *Old House Farm* in woodland. Walk behind the ruin and descend steeply around a small coombe and then more gently through the wood. After a boggy area walk up to the edge of the wood and continue along the edge of the field to a road.

Cross to a gate alongside *Coronation Cottage* and follow the track to an old barn, turn right alongside a fence down to a stile, and continue down the field to the road. Cross over and descend, half left, to a stream and then climb the opposite side to the chapel at Knightwick. Walk through the cemetery to a lane, turn left down to the road again and cross to a footpath which contours to the right, above a house, through undergrowth and then a gate. Cross a final field to the Worcester - Bromyard road at Knightwick.

Although not on the most direct line between Hereford and Worcester, Knightwick is the most convenient crossing of the Teme for the Three Choirs Way. The river is also a symbolic boundary between Welsh Herefordshire and English Worcestershire.
The Teme, rising in the Welsh hills flows past hop yards and orchards, farmsteads and hamlets, through the rich valley below the Abberley hills before rounding Ankerdine Hill towards the Severn.

Walk down 100 yards and cross, *joining the Worcestershire Way,* to the old road through the village which provides a footway over the River Teme to the Talbot Inn. Continue uphill, signposted to Martley. The pavement ends as the road steepens, and around a corner turn right onto a footpath alongside a house into the wood. Follow the garden boundary, turning left and climbing parallel with the road. At a path junction turn right, more steeply uphill, still with the Worcestershire Way.

At the top of the steep section avoid a path cutting back left and continue alongside a pallisade around a house, until reaching the ridge path and turn left. The path becomes a track, continue for about 300 yards, through a white gate at the wood edge. The Worcestershire Way continues northwards, but the Three Choirs Way turns sharp right, alongside a house, down a green track which becomes a pleasant hollow way.

Emerging from the woodland at a junction ignore the track forking right, and continue down the hollow way to a brick and clapboard barn. Over a stile descend steeply to follow a small valley curving right to a further stile, cross and turn left down a surfaced driveway. At the bottom keep left and turn left through a farm gate at Bannersbrook. Walk up to a field gate, immediately left of a red brick building, and continue uphill at the edge of a wood.

As the woodland falls away continue up until close to a hedge, and turn left to a gate. Through this, angle away from the fence on the left, to a gate, just left of a white cottage on to Easinghope Lane.

This country differs from dry uplands, water hereabouts
is no white rarity. The muddy ditch
the Saxons named still moves beside the road
and milking-time soon churns the yard to sludge.

Men could build where they would; farms
five fields apart and cottages in threes up tracks
now detail slope and hollow, and lanes mizmaze
the countryside, hedges a screen for lover and for fox.

Thorn, hazel, briar make them alike, easy
to lose one's way, different in small things only -
empty beehives in a gangling orchard, a church
with no apparent parish, shock-yewed and lonely.

Sometimes these lanes go by, irrelevant as thoughts,
for miles with only magpies, padlocked gate, and crop,
a philosophic pattern to the man born locally,
to others only metaphors without a map.

Molly Holden

Turn right down the lane to a junction, near renovated oast-houses, at Doddenham. Turn left alongside a wall for a few yards to a footpath on the right. Fork left to a gate up a short slope, and then walk down alongside a hedge before turning left along the valley bottom.

Through an old boundary hedge continue to a hedge corner and follow a ditch and old willow trees to a field gate. Continue on the same line, passing under power lines, to a further gate onto a lane.

Turn right for about 50 yards to a footpath along a track on the left. Follow this, parallel to power lines, and through a gateway continue along the edge of a wood for about 100 yards. As the wood edge and power lines turn left, continue straight on to a stile and footbridge in woodland.

In the next field, incline right and follow the hedge line over stiles to *Broad Green.* Cross a road and follow the edge of the village green to a lane on the left, signed No Through Road. This soon becomes a rough track, and after a 100 yards, turn right over a stile and follow a headland path towards woodland.

At the field corner, turn right for 50 yards and then left to a pedestrian gate, sometimes hidden in undergrowth. Through this emerge into an open field alongside a wood. Follow the wood edge to the left, over three stiles, some of which may be hidden by overgrowth. After the third stile, turn right, and follow the hedge past the remains of *Blackfield Cottage* and a pond on the left. At the corner, do not continue over a stile, but turn left to a further stile and cross this keeping the hedge to the right.

From the next stile, walk down the field parallel to the hedge to the right. Cross a footbridge and stile in a wire fence and walk through a row of oak trees, marking an old boundary, to a stile in the corner adjacent to a small enclosure. Continue with the hedge to the left to a further stile, and then cross a short field to a footbridge and handgate. Again follow the hedge on the left to the corner and go through the left of two gates, then turn right over a footbridge and stile.

Walk along the edge of two fields, and after the second leave the hedge and angle up the field, left of red-brick houses, to a gate on to the road at Upper Broadheath. Turn right and, after a cross-road, walk along the edge of the Common in preference to the road for about 400 yards to the Plough Inn. A few yards further turn left along a bridleway alongside Elgar's birthplace.

Elgar was born at The Firs, Lower Broadheath, and the cottage is now a museum, housing a collection of priceless manuscripts, including many of his original scores. The cottage has a very welcoming aura, Elgar often alluded to this and his awareness that 'music is in the air around you'.

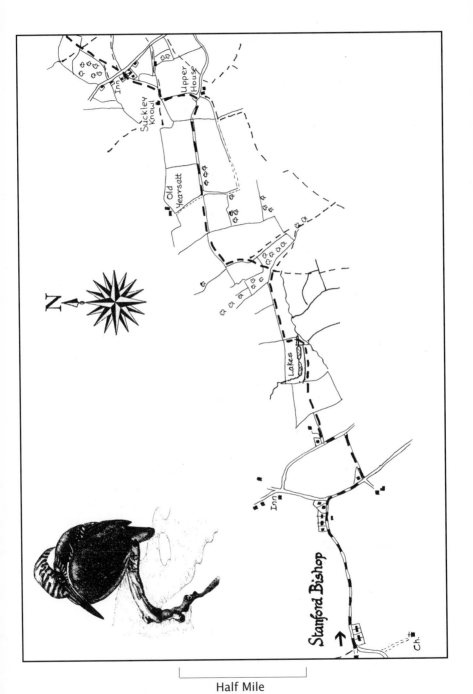

Half Mile

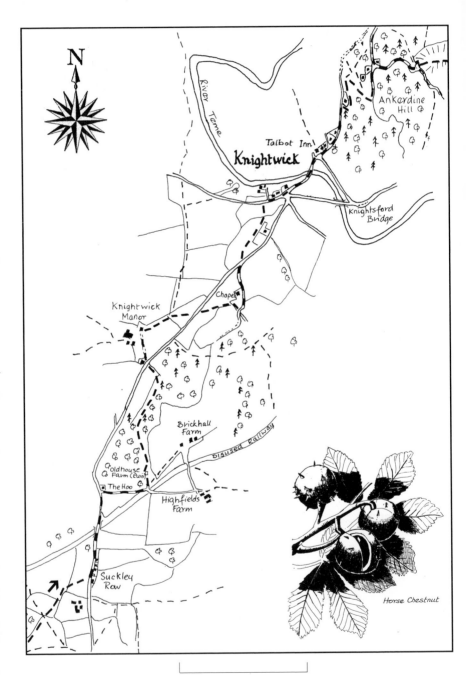

N

River Teme

Talbot Inn
Knightwick

Ankerdine Hill

Knightsford Bridge

Chapel

Knightwick Manor

Brickhall Farm

Disused Railway

Goldhouse Farm (Ruin)

The Hoo

Highfields Farm

Suckley Row

Horse Chestnut

Half Mile

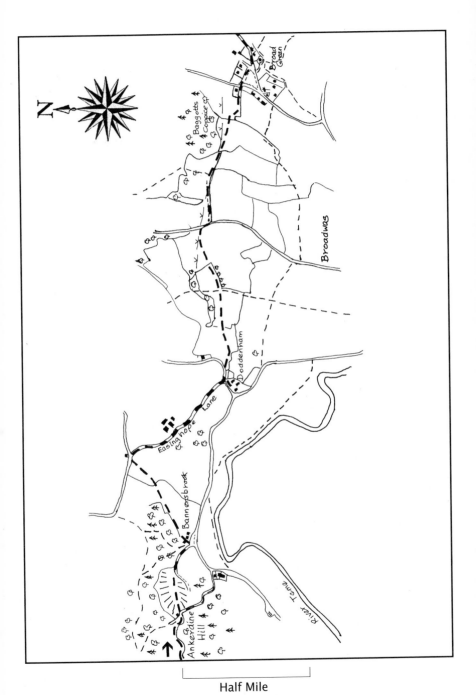

Half Mile

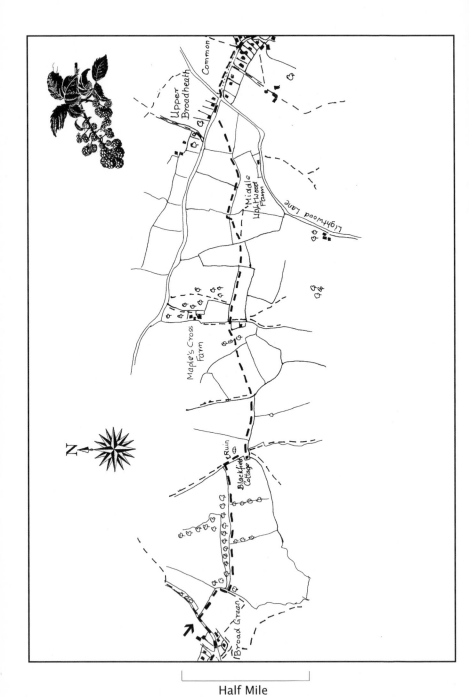

Common

Upper Broadheath

Middle Highwood Farm

Lightwood Lane

Maple's Cross Farm

Ruin

Blackfeet Cottage

Broad Green

N

Half Mile

Broadheath to Malvern Link

Follow the track for about half a mile to Oldbury Farm and after two bridlegates continue directly towards Worcester cathedral ahead. *The bulk of Bredon Hill looms and beyond is the high blue edge of Cotswold. To the right, the Malvern ridge extends southwards.*

The bridleway soon becomes a surfaced lane and at a sharp bend joins Oldbury Road which is followed for about a mile and a half to the banks of the Severn. Any tedium of walking through the suburbs may be relieved at the *Copper Top Inn*. Otherwise continue, and none too soon, cross Henwyck Road and descend Holywell Hill to the west bank of the Severn. Walk right for 200 yards to the *Sabrina* footbridge, and cross the river.

Turn right on the riverside path, part of the Severn Way long distance path, shortly cross the end of Worcester Bridge and continue pleasantly alongside the river passing the Glovers's Needle. *This slender spire of St Andrew's, rising to 245 feet, commemorates the Worcester glove trade, which up to 1800 gave employment to 8000 people in the city and surrounding countryside.*

After 300 yards the medieval *Portway* leads up to the Cathedral, and the city centre. *Note the floodwater levels on the embankment which show why the Three Choirs Way may not be accessible at all times of the year!*

Completed in 1998, the Severn Way runs for 220 miles, along or near the river, from the source on Plynlimon to the sea. A mountain torrent in parts of Powys the river meanders through Shropshire and Worcestershire past historic scenes and ancient communities. The river changes from tree bordered tranquillity at Tewkesbury, to a mile wide tidal estuary at Sheperdine before joining the Bristol Channel.

The Severn is Britains longest river. Rising in the mountains of mid Wales, close to the source of the Wye, the two rivers enclose a tract of countryside as attractive as any in the country, aptly described as 'blessed is the eye between Severn and Wye'.

A crucial trade route for centuries, by the 1600's the Severn was the second busiest river in Europe, after the Meuse. In 1701 there was a regular water taxi between Shrewsbury and Gloucester, and , by the middle of the 18th Century, 100,000 tons of coal was shipped down the river from Coalport annually. Severn Trows of up to 80 tons laden, plied both up and downstream to adjacent Midland towns, the Bristol Channel ports, and beyond.

The city arose around a major ford when the Severn was still tidal up to this point. The strong Saxon influence - the west Saxons here were prominent in the defeat of the Danes- led to the Shire system developing in England. In the Fifth Century Worcester was the fifth city in the land.

After Norman Conquest Worcester was the only diocese to retain a Saxon Bishop, Wulfstan.

King John visited Worcester in 1206 claiming it to be his favourite city and in his will requested burial there. He is said to have been influenced by a prophesy, attributed to Merlin, that he would eventually rest among Saints. Subsequently, his tomb between that of St Oswald and St Wulfstan led to Worcester becoming a centre of pilgrimage, with resulting wealth, a century before Gloucester found similar fame and fortune.

The Civil War began and ended at Worcester. In 1642 Charles I was recruiting in the area, generally loyal to him, when a skirmish at Powick Bridge resulted in the Parliamentary Force being routed by Royal Cavalry.
During the fluctuating fortunes of the Civil War, Worcester remained under a Royal garrison until blockaded by the Roundheads New Model Army in 1651. Cromwells 'Crowning Mercy', the destruction of city's massive walls, 50' high, was the last action of the Civil War.

John Wesley looked with affection on "our lovely and loving people of Worcester, plain, old genuine Methodists"!

William Cobbett, touring agricultural England in 1826, found it "one of the cleanest, neatest and handsomest towns I ever saw, indeed I do not recollect to have seen any one equal....the town is precisely in character with the beautiful and rich country in which it lies".
Modern Town Planning has not been so appreciative, and the character which Cobbett saw in the City changed drastically.

Elgar lived with his parents in Worcester from 1859 to 1879, where his fathers music shop was at 10 High Street. After the death of his wife Elgar returned to live in Kempsey near Worcester from 1929 until his death in 1934.

Continue, southwards, on the Severn Way for over two miles, passing the entrance to the Birmingham canal at Diglis Basin, and shortly afterward Diglis locks. After a length of rural riverside a side stream blocks the way. Follow the stream inland to a footbridge and over this, return to the river bank and continue southwards.

Soon, after passing the confluence of the Teme and Severn opposite, walk through a caravan site, and then under a road bridge, and leave the river bank by a graded path up to the roadside at Timberdine roundabout. *The Ketch Inn is about 200 yards away back towards the city.*

There was Welsh in the English water
That flowed from distant mountains
Where high on Plynlimon springs the Hafren.
There hawk, the buzzard and the merlin,
Westward hovers Cader Idris
And the silver Dovey.
The rushing stream passes
Through peat and pool,
Waterfall and cascade,
Spouts to Llyn Crochan,
Then sliding to Blaen Hafren
Becomes the Severn.

. . . To enter gorge and wood
To wind by castle, hill, and valley,
Meander through remote pastures
Then race through towns and under bridges
To Bewdley, Stourport, Worcester, . . .
Past Callow End, past Kempsey church
That looks from its hill across the Ham
Over shoals and willows to the Old Hills
And the blue line of the Malverns.
Downstream lie Severn Stoke and Pixham Ferry,
Its rusted chains now vanished,
No longer used to haul across the hunt.
Farther down lie Upton,
Ripple with its misericords . . .
Then Tewkesbury, Gloucester,
The estuary and the Bristol Channel. . .

Robin Ivy

Cross Timberdine bridge, and after about 300 yards turn left down a concrete slip road back towards the river. At the bottom, go through a gate and turn right along a fence for 40 yards to a further gate into the river meadows. Angling away from power lines on the right walk close to two large oak trees, to a gateway and farm bridge in the next boundary.

Continue in the next field for about 100 yards on a line converging with a stream on the left to a gate. Through the next long field, waymarks indicate a route, on slightly higher ground, close to the stream. As the stream and power lines begin to converge turn left over a stile and a footbridge into an enclosed track.

After a path junction, the green lane nears a house and the right of way diverts over a footbridge on the right, and along the field headland to a stile. Continue up a field passing a noduled oak tree, and a stile to the left and from the next hedge angle right, past another large oak, to a stile onto a road.

Cross the road with care, as foliage may obscure you from approaching drivers, and enter an enclosed path through a metal kissing gate and pass Stanbrook Abbey on the other side of the hedge. At the path end emerge close to Callow End, *calwa - bare hillside, a reference to nearby Old Hills which are still largely bare of trees.*

The village was a centre of hop growing up to the 1950's and itinerant pickers used to descend on the village in considerable numbers. The Bluebell Inn is a quarter of a mile.

The barley grows with modest head,
The hop is all ambition,
But when in barrels they are wed
The mixture is perfection.
Hail to thee, Worcestershire!

George Griffith

Turn right along a lane between a hedge and high brick wall for about 300 yards. As the lane curves left continue over a stile and along an enclosed green track which climbs to join a hard track alongside a barn.

Carry straight on to the ridge top, *with views to Powick Church.* The path diverts past a cottage, downhill to a stile and choice of paths. Turn left alongside a hedge, under oak trees and through a gate alongside a small stable.

Continue up the next paddock to a stile and follow any route to the summit of Old Hills and a splendid panorama. *North, the Cathedral and 'The Glovers Needle' are prominent, and further east the Severn Vale. In the west the Suckley Hills are overshadowed by North Hill, at the end of the Malvern ridge.*

From the Trig. point, conversely set just below the highest point, walk down a broad path but fork left within a few yards. At the bottom of the slope cross a stile and follow a headland to a stile into the woodland. At a cross path turn right and at the next cross path left and follow this to a stile out of the wood. Turn right over a stile alongside a gate and turn left along a hedge to a gate and a stream. Through the gate turn right along a headland outside the wood and continue along the wooded banks of the stream for about a mile.

Approaching the parkland around Madresfield Court angle away slightly from the stream and a stile in the corner to a gate, and join a surfaced lane. Walk beneath varied mature trees to a road alongside the decorative Lodge, with a particularly splendid chimney. *Madresfield Court is mentioned in a charter of Henry I. It has been occupied by descendants of the same family since 1160.*

Turn left, and after 50 yards cross the road to a path through a gate. Over a stile cross the field, in line with North Hill, to a second stile. Walk straight on along a farm track to a gate and continue alongside a lake to a stile into woodland, and follow the wood edge to a road. Cross to a path up the middle of a field. *Called 'Little Black Crofts' on 1840 Tithe Map. The hedge on the left is the remnant of medieval woodland and contains a few wild service trees, once a common native species, the numbers are dwindling rapidly.*

Cross a fence by a flimsy stile and a short enclosed path leads to a new road. Cross this and follow a path through a new area of light industry, *once 'The Old Hopyard',* over another service road, continue along a field edge and fork left around an electricity sub-station. Turn right over a concrete slab footbridge and follow the enclosed path around to the front of the sub- station. Turn left and walk up the access road, branching left at a junction, and continue, past a sports field on the right, to a T junction.

Cross over, slightly right, to an enclosed path between holly hedges and cross the next road to Malvern Link Common. *A seat encircling a hawthorn tree may provide a brief respite.* Follow a broad path uphill inclining left though trees and shrubbery to an underpass through the Hereford to Worcester railway embankment. Cross a narrow road and continue up the steepening Common, still inclining left, to the Nags Head Inn and then walk up adjacent Bank Street at Malvern Link.

Emerge onto North Malvern Road beneath the steep slopes of North Hill. Cross the road and turn left along the elevated footway, for about 300 yards, to an unsigned footpath on the right. *Access to the path is inside a private looking drive and might easily be missed. A guide is Oriel House, with the ornate pinnacles, on the opposite side of the road. Enter the driveway and cross to steep stone steps, signed North Hill.*

Malvern Town Council has recently taken over the maintainence of their footpaths from the County Council. They have expressed enthusiasm for the Three Choirs Way and will no doubt bring about improvements for walkers, including, perhaps, a signpost for this footpath.

Urban Malvern clusters at different levels along the eastern flank of the hills, spreading south from North Malvern through Malvern Link to the centre of Great Malvern, set below Worcestershire Beacon.

Slightly detached, and almost half way down the length of the ridge, is Malvern Wells, where Holy Well derived its name from miraculous cures attributed to bathing in the water, and the Eye Well is recorded as 'curing sore eyes' in 1622.

Malvern water has been famous for centuries. Springs all over Europe are famous for their mineral content but Malvern water is reputed for its purity.

The small cottage at St Ann's Well, built in 1815, is a memorial to the 'village spa' which existed before the cures attracted national acclaim, and brought the large houses, hotels and the Promenade Gardens. In 1781 the water sold in London at one shilling a bottle and it is still bottled and marketed commercially from St Johns Well.

After his marriage in 1889, Edward Elgar and his wife lived in the London area for two, fairly unproductive years. In 1891 they returned to live in Great Malvern, firstly in Alexandra Road and then in Wells Road, where Elgar's study overlooked the wide panorama of the Severn Vale.

The hills, over which Elgar regularly wandered, were a constant source of inspiration to him and he completed the 'Enigma Variations', 'The Dream of Gerontius', and the 'Pomp and Circumstance Marches' during this period.

The Malvern Hills, consisting of exceptionally hard rock which has resisted natural erosion for at least 650 million years, run north - south for nearly 10 miles, rising to a height of 1394 feet at Worcester Beacon. Much of the ridge is dry grassland with patches of bilberry and heather and is designated an Area of Outstanding Natural Beauty.

The hills are protected by law incorporating a Board of Conservators who manage and maintain the environment of the hills and surrounding commons, a major function being the preservation of public accessibility. Fewer sheep now graze the hills than previously, allowing woodland and scrub to extend, while regular, managed, burning brings fresh growth with a legacy of native wildflowers, including bluebells and foxgloves. Lower slopes are clad in low scrub, blackberry, bracken, broom and gorse with areas of woodland consisting of silver birch, mountain ash, hawthorn, sycamore and, lower still, oak.

The entire area, including the adjoining commons, is open to the public and criss crossed by a network of paths and tracks estimated at more than 100 miles in extent. Through walkers, and first time visitors, may wish to walk the backbone of the ridge. Others will prefer lower levels, walking through primrose and bluebells in spring and tree shade in summer, or taking the waters at St Anne's Well.

Hop vine

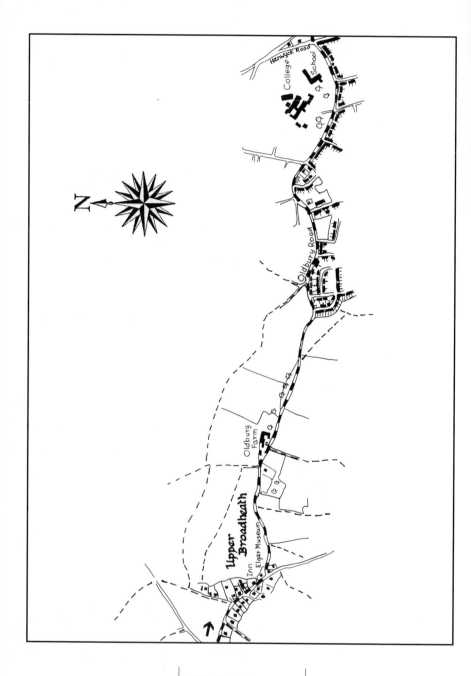

Half Mile

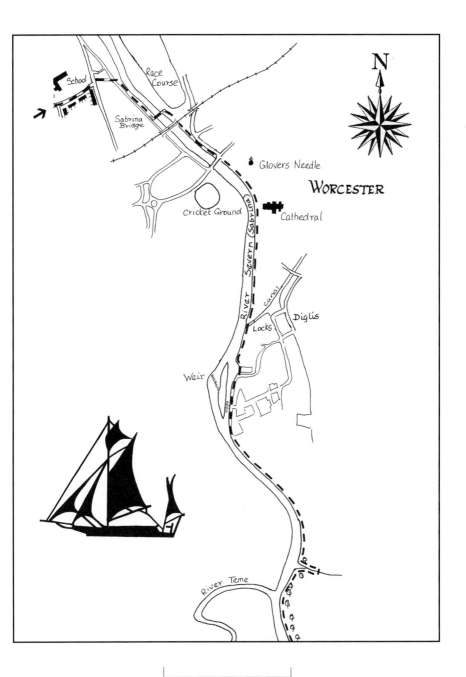

Half Mile

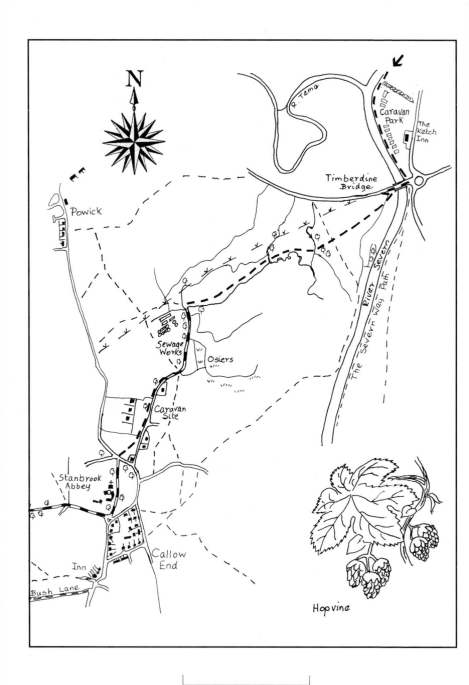

N

R. Tama

Caravan Park

The Ketch Inn

Timberdine Bridge

Powick

The Severn Way Path

River Severn

Sewage Works

Osiers

Caravan Site

Stanbrook Abbey

Callow End

Inn

Bush Lane

Hop vine

Half Mile

Reproduced by kind permission of Ordnance Survey © Crown Copyright MC/99-073

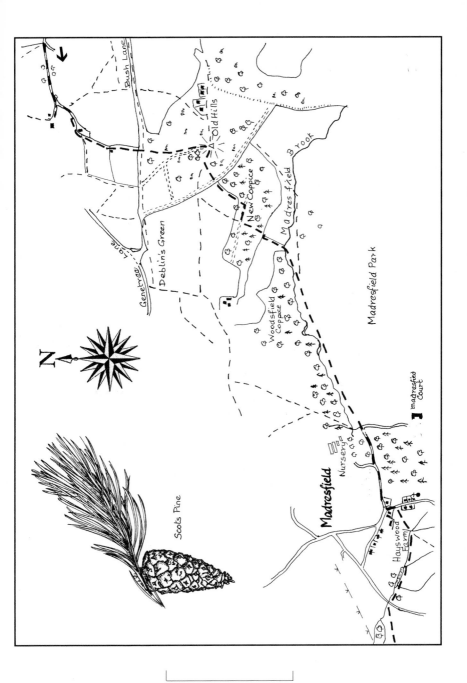

N

Bush Lane

Old Hills

Madresfield Brook

New Coppice

Madresfield Park

Geneva Lane

Deblin's Green

Woodsfield Coppice

Madresfield Court

Madresfield

Nursery

Hayswood Farm

Scots Pine

Half Mile

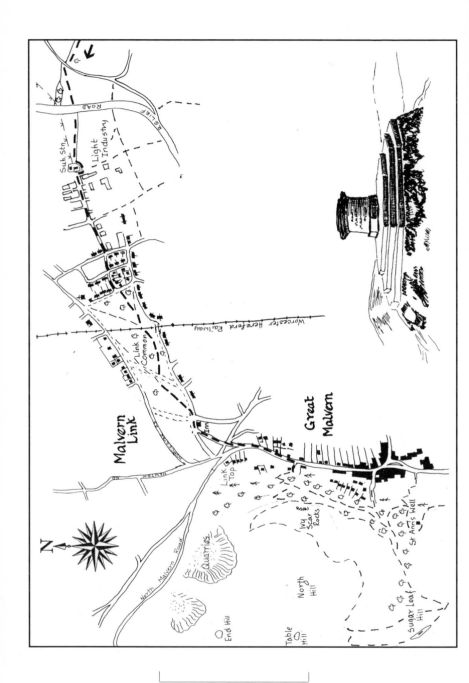

Half Mile

Malvern Link to Pendock

It is difficult to describe, coherently, any particular route in detail, particularly on the open grassy contours and at path junctions. Many paths parallel each other at different levels along the hillsides allowing routes to be chosen as desired.

Whether visiting the Toposcope on Worcester Beacon or not, the ridge is followed south for about two miles, to Wyche Cutting, *route of an old Salt Way from Droitwich,* followed by a further three miles to British Camp, the extensive hill fort on Hereford Beacon, second highest point along the ridge.

.... "twelve fair counties saw the glare from Malverns lonely peak" , according to MacCauley in his historic Armada poem. Others claim as many as fifteen. However many, the panorama is magnificent and on a clear day extends over much of the three counties.
Eastwards across the Severn vale, over Worcestershire and Gloucestershire to the blue Cotswold horizon. Southward the lower Severn and the Bristol Channel show clearly.
While in the west the undulating and well wooded hills of Herefordshire advance in waves to the mountains of Brecon and Radnor.

THE THREE CHOIRS WAY

The Shire Ditch is a prominent feature of the ridge top. In 1290 Gilbert de Clare, Earl of Gloucester constructed this boundary between his land and that of the Bishop of Hereford. Craftily, it was said, so that deer could jump easily from west to east but with considerably more difficulty the opposite way!

The ridge narrows to the pass at British Camp below, at Little Malvern the remains of the Benedictine Priory can be glimpsed.

William Langland was born at Ledbury and educated at Little Malvern Priory where he may have written part of his famous allegorical poem "The vision of Piers Plowman". From the Norman Conquest the Saxon tongue was declining and soon, with much of France owing allegiance to England, French nobility and their entourages were commonplace at the English Court. After 250 years the two languages were beginning to coalesce. Langland's literature was part of an important revival of the native tongue, and his idiomatic use of English was the base for the language of Shakespeare.

From British Camp continue for a mile along the ridge, or on a lower path above the reservoir, to Hangmans Hill. Descend to a col, where the link path from the Gloucestershire Way climbs up from the east, and the Worcestershire Way passes through woodland to the west. The ridge continues, interrupted by the steep valley at *The Gullet*, old quarry workings and intruding roads, to Midsummer Hill.

It is more straightforward, and equally rewarding, to join the Worcestershire Way on the western flank, descending through Gullet Wood. At a junction with a path leading to the *Obelisk* overlooking Eastnor Park, continue up the flank of Midsummer Hill followed by a gradual descent to Hollybush, and the termination of the Worcestershire Way.

From Hollybush carpark turn left along the Ledbury - Tewkesbury road and, over the crest, descend for about 200 yards, to a track on the right just before a telephone kiosk. The track bends left and then climbs the shoulder of Ragged Stone hill curving right, before levelling out through deciduous woodland. After 350 yards or so leave this pleasant way and turn left down to an obvious gate.

Walk down the open field, angling right about 45 degrees, to a track and follow this to the right. *Used freely for many years as a right of way, this track, and others nearby, do not appear on the Definitive Map.* Through a gate, the track continues pleasantly through thick woodland, crossing over a narrow road to Whiteleaved Oak, by a hardly noticed bridge. Continue for half a mile, to a point where the track, bending left, commences to curve right, and turn left on a track descending from the right, down to a field gate. Walk down the headland *with wide views to Bredon Hill and the Cotswold outliers. The view further south is obscured by Lyce's Coppice on a hillock a quarter of a mile away.*

At the road, *Chase End Street* turn right, and passing a turning to *Camer's Green*, walk to a right hand bend near a black and white timbered cottage. Turn left through a gateway, and follow the wide headland.

Established by William the Conqueror in 1083, as Royal Hunting Forest, Malvern Chase extended as heath and woodland from the Severn,

Where this bends right, go through the gap in the hedge ahead and behind a pond. Follow the hedge, now on the right, to a footbridge. *This field is often wet and more than thirty small ponds, shown on the OS map in the vicinity, are indicative of this.* From the bridge walk up the field, angling slightly right, towards a line of four oak trees and a slightly raised track leading to a gate onto a road.

Turn right for about 200 yards, to a footpath through a gate on the left.

Walk alongside the hedge to a cross boundary and turn right over a stile. Bypass a barn on the path, through a gate, and continue down the headland to a further stile. Over this a path is often left clear of crops alongside the coppice and pond on the right, down to a gate to the right of a house, onto a road. Turn left along *Cook's Lane* for half a mile, and then right at a junction, continue for another half mile, passing under the M5 motorway and alongside the *Wyndbrook,* to a T junction and turn left towards Pendock, *which has a shop and Post Office.*

Beech

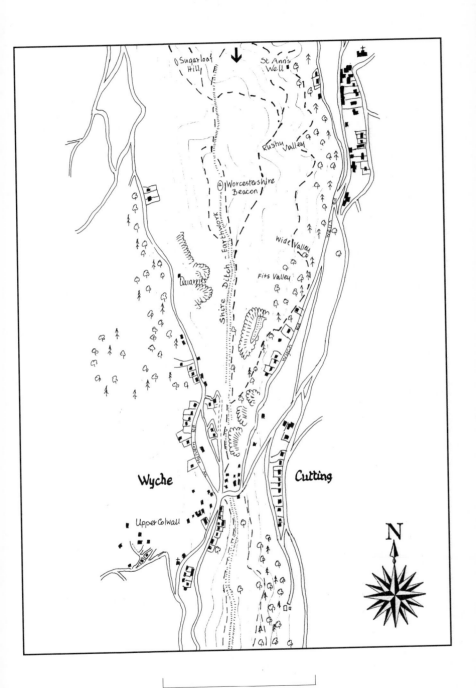

Sugarloaf Hill

St Ann's Well

Rushy Valley

Worcestershire Beacon

Wide Valley

Shire Ditch — Earthwork

Fits Valley

Quarries

Wyche   Cutting

Upper Colwall

N

Half Mile

Reproduced by kind permission of Ordnance Survey © Crown Copyright MC/99-073

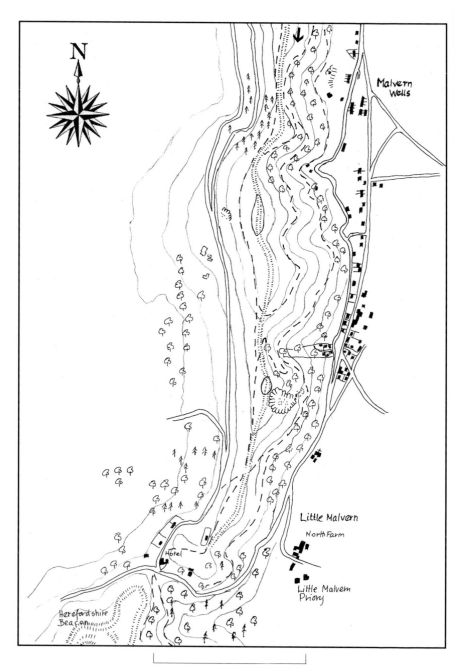

Half Mile

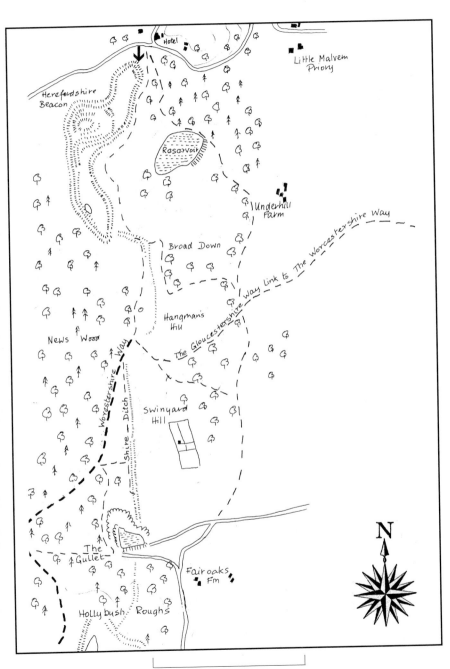

Half Mile

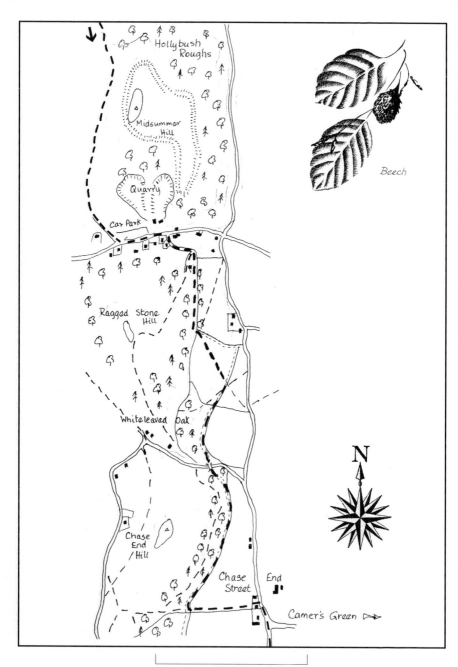

Hollybush
Roughs

Midsummer
Hill

Quarry

Car Park

Ragged Stone
Hill

Whiteleaved Oak

Chase
End
Hill

Chase
Street

End

Camer's Green ⟹

Beech

N

Half Mile

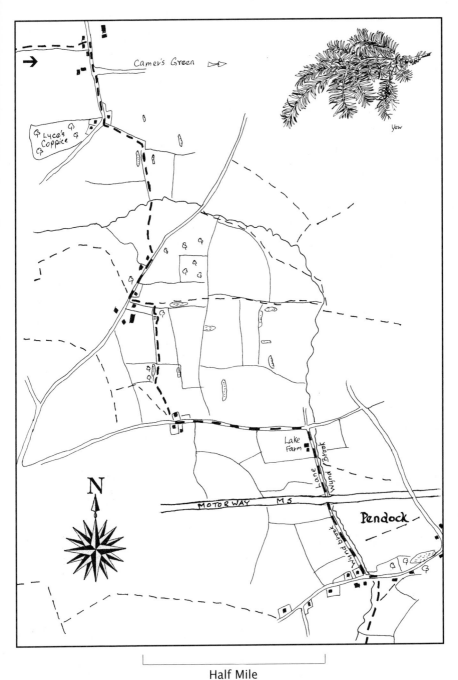

Camer's Green ➤➤

Luce's Coppice

Yew

N

Lake Farm

Lane

Wynd Brook

MOTORWAY M5

Pendock

Wynd Brook

Half Mile

Pendock to Gloucester

Within 50 yards, turn right through a fieldgate and walk, parallel to the hedge on the right to a gate and continue towards a further gate. Just before reaching this turn left, cross a footbridge, and walk up the next field alongside the hedge, turning right at the top of the slope.

The wide view from this vantage point includes a glimpse of May Hill summit over the trees in front, and Gadsbury Hill off to the left, its ancient fortifications shrouded by the tree cover. Cross a stile and continue alongside young poplars bordering a fruit tree nursery, to a road at Dobshill Farm.

Turn right for 20 yards and then left into the ungated farm yard, with two red brick barns on the left. The track bends left, under a horse chestnut tree to a gate, and keeping to the right of it, follow a splendid headland path along a ridge. To *the left, beyond Gadsbury Hill, is the conicular shape of Berth Hill, with Eldersfield Church spire prominent between them.*

Continue for three quarters of a mile, passing stiles on the right, to a hunt gate. Turn left and follow the boundary down, beneath more

Chestnut trees, and through the right hand of two gates. Turn right and follow the hedge, *with an imposing Gothic pile on the other side of the hedge, once Staunton vicarage.*

Cross a lane, and continue, rising towards Staunton Coppice, to a gate onto a farm track. Follow this to the left for 100 yards and then turn right through a gate. Walk parallel to the coppice to another gate under an oak tree, and continue alongside the hedge bordering the wood. *Be alert to turn right over a stile through the hedge at the end of the coppice before reaching the field end.*

Turn left, into an enclosed path alongside a garden and bungalow, to a junction with a stoned track. Turn right, and where the track turns left, continue along an enclosed grassy path, passing a bungalow and outbuildings, and sometimes tethered goats. *Once the meeting place of Chartists, a short lived group which extolled equality and enfranchisement, for all, long before such radical ideas became accepted.*

Cross a stile, *waymarked as part of the Whitmore Way, a local short circular route,* and turn left onto a cross bridleway. Go through a hunt gate, along an enclosed length to *Moat Lane* and turn right, to the Gloucester - Ledbury road at Staunton.

Turn left for 100 yards and cross the road to a footbridge. A short enclosed path, followed by three stiles through paddocks, lead to new housing where the path now follows the access road through Collingham Close. Turn left at the next two junctions and shortly pass the Prince of Wales Inn. At a T junction turn right for 150 yards and then left, signposted *'School Crescent - No Through Road'*

At the road end climb a stile into a field and continue straight on, converging with the hedge on the left after about 100 yards. Go through a gap in a cross hedge near a large oak tree, and continue, still with the hedge on the left, over a foot bridge and after the next field, a stile alongside a gate. Now with hedge on the right walk to another stile and then cross a field to the corner where a stile and footbridge lead on to the Gloucester- Upton on Severn road.

Cross over to a gate, and walk up the field to a further stile, and continue steeply up alongside Corse Wood. At the top go through a gate on the left, again with a stile alongside, and turn right following the hedge downhill for about 200 yards to a stile. Over this continue down, now with the hedge to the left, to a gate onto a lane.

Turn right, and after about 50 yards, left on a footpath down the driveway at *Ivy Cottage*. As the drive bends left to the cottage, walk straight on, past a garage and between vegetable plots to a stile. Bear left to a further stile, over this continue with the hedge to the left. After 150 yards or so fork left through a gate near an electricity pole. *Barrow Hill imitates May Hill in profile. Further off Sandhurst Hill above the Severn stands out against the blue line of the Cotswolds.*

Follow the electricity poles down to a stile immediately right of the farmhouse, *Rio Candy Ranch, someone's dream of rural living ?* Turn right along the lane for 40 yards and left through a gate on a bridleway and cross the field to a further gate. The bridleway forks left after 20 yards, but continue straight on, down a good track, with the hedge to the left. At the bottom of this field continue with the track and hedge bending left, through a stand of Poplars and past the remains of Foscombe Farm. *Foscombe House, a Gothic extravaganza built by Thomas Fulljames in 1840, can be glimpsed on Foscombe Hill up to the right.*

The track passes through a converging hedge. After about 100 yards, at a path junction, turn left over the stream, and then immediately right following it. Cross a stile and walk along the field where the growth of abundant ash and willow trees obscures surrounding views, other than Sandhurst Hill in front, seemingly very close over the trees.
Pass a field gate on the right, and after another 150 yards, just prior to

electricity lines, turn right through a farm gate and over a culvert. Walk up the field, moving away from the hedge slightly, to a stile. Walk through a coppice and follow either of two public paths which cross the playing field, passing either in front or behind the white painted pavilion. Turn right along an enclosed path between houses to a road, and turn left to a T junction in the centre of Ashleworth.

While there are numerous footpaths in the vicinity of the village few lead satisfactorily towards Gloucester. Two routes are suitable for the Three Choirs Way, but in the event of winter flooding neither will be feasible, and it would be necessary to stay on the road from Ashleworth along the ridge to Maisemore.

Alternative Route following the Severn.
From the T junction, cross to the right of the Post Office and walk down a track for a few yards. Where a path crosses turn over the stile on the right. Walk diagonally down the field, passing left of a row of trees, including *Field Maple, Black Poplar, Cherry, Copper Beech , Lime and Hornbeam*.
Through a gap in the corner continue on the same line to the next corner and a stile. Over this walk down the headland to a lane. Turn right to a junction where a stalwart signpost indicates the direction to Ashleworth Quay, where opposite the pub a bridleway follows the river bank towards Gloucester.

When the towpath was in commercial use it followed the eastern bank from Gloucester Docks. The confluence with the River Chelt and Wainlode cliff upstream of the pub necessitated the towpath changing banks. The Boat Inn provided refreshment for boatmen at the point where a chain ferry transferred the horses across the river. The medieval Ashleworth Court and Tithe Barn, which is 40 yards long, are built of limestone, whereas the Manor House is a timber framed building. The church and surroundings are often flooded.

From the T junction turn right through the village passing the Queens Arms, and a road to the left. Continue around bends to a junction with Longridge Lane and follow this. *Unfortunately it is not along the ridge, where it would provide a splendid approach to the City, but along the foot of the slope. Although it is a pleasant and ancient way, views are restricted.*

Pass two cottages, one thatched, and in a further 200 yards note a bridleway on the right. This climbs up to the ridge and could be utilised in the event of the riverside ahead being impassable. Continue past Longridge Farm, through a gate into an open field, and follow the left hand boundary. From the next gateway fork diagonally right to the riverbank and follow it for half a mile. *Called the Long Reach, this is straight length of the river to Maisemore, possibly relates to the days of sail, when Severn Trows, particularly going north, might have had a brief sail on the prevailing winds.*

At a cross hedge and stream follow the bridleway turning right up the hill to Home Farm. The optional route from Ashleworth and the Boat Inn continues along the river bank and might be preferable, river conditions permitting, in the future. Minor obstructions, which had existed for some years, are to be removed as the result of a Public Inquiry, which found that any erosion of the river bank had not extinguished the public way.

Pass *Maisemore Park,* hidden from prying eyes, as is the view of Gloucester, by the high hedge, and continue to a junction and bear left. Maisemore Church on its hill comes into view on the right, and rounding a bend, the Cathedral appears against the background of Robinswood Hill and the Cotswold scarp.

Who says 'Gloucester' sees a tall
Fair fashioned shape of stone arise,
That changes with the changing skies
From joy to funereal gloom......

The surprising, the enormous Severn Plain
So wide, so fair
From Crickley seen or Cooper's, my dear lane
That holds all lane delightfulnesses there
O Maisemore's darling way !

Ivor Gurney

*Ivor Gurney was born at Gloucester in 1890. A fellow chorister
and student with Herbert Howells he was a great friend of Will
Harvey of Minsterworth. Largely unrecognised during his short
lifetime, his songs, based mainly on the work of English poets,
are pastoral, reflective and melodious. He set few of his own
poems to music, but these portray the pleasant countryside around
Gloucester which he loved to ramble through.*

Walk through Maisemore to the Gloucester - Ledbury road outside the
White Hart Inn, *where a celebratory drink to the Three Choirs Way
might justifiably be in order?*

*Maes Mawr -a great field. This may have referred to Alney Island,
which is enclosed by the two arms of the Severn and extends for
more than two miles from Maisemore to the city.*

Turn left towards Gloucester over Maisemore bridge and passing a
bridleway signpost and a roadside cross, continue for 100 yards to a
footpath through a gateway on the left.
Angle right across the corner of the field to a stile and continue on the
same line crossing two further fields. After the third boundary walk
beneath electricity power lines to converge with the hedge on the left at
a footbridge.

Still on the same line, continue to the bank of the Severn's eastern channel. Follow this to the right beneath the orbital road around the west of the city, to a stile. Over this turn right to a footbridge and further stile and then walk left along the boundary of the *Irish Associations Hurling Pitch,* and through the railway viaduct. *Where you last were a few days, or months, ago, according to your expediency since setting out on the Three Choirs Way.*

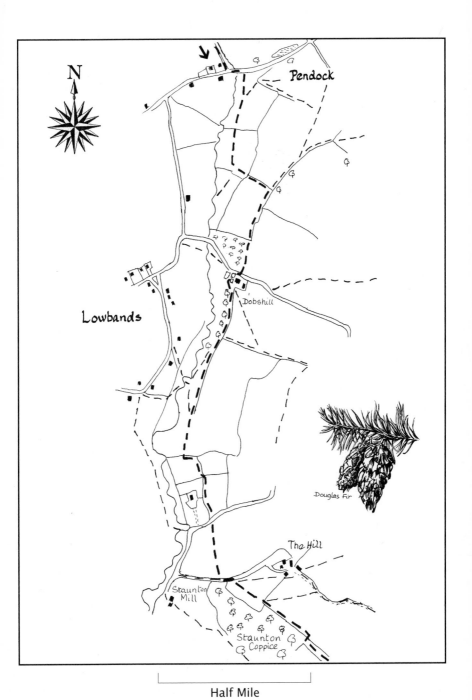

N

Pendock

Lowbands

Dobshill

Douglas Fir

The Hill

Staunton Mill

Staunton Coppice

Half Mile

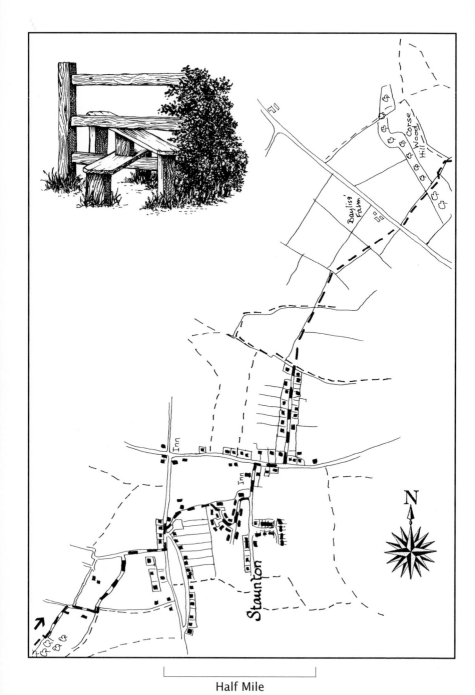

Half Mile

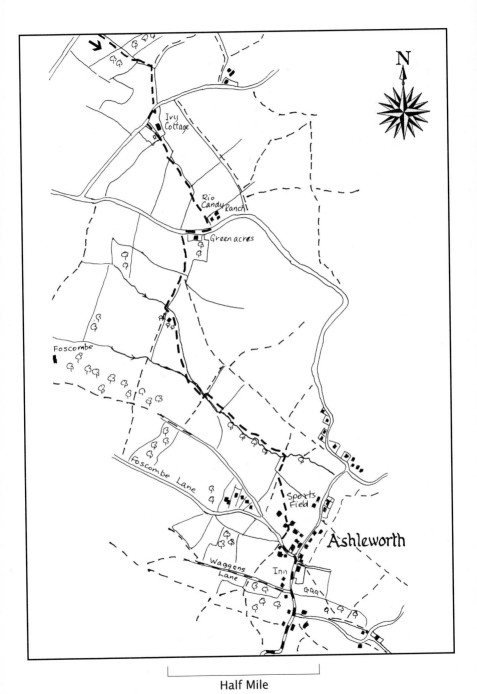

N

Ivy Cottage

Rio Candy Ranch

Greenacres

Foscombe

Foscombe Lane

Sports Field

Ashleworth

Waggons Lane

Inn

Half Mile

Reproduced by kind permission of Ordnance Survey © Crown Copyright MC/99-073

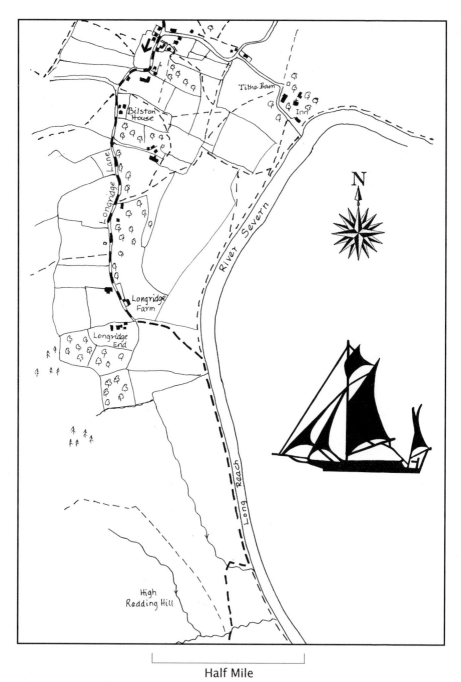

Half Mile

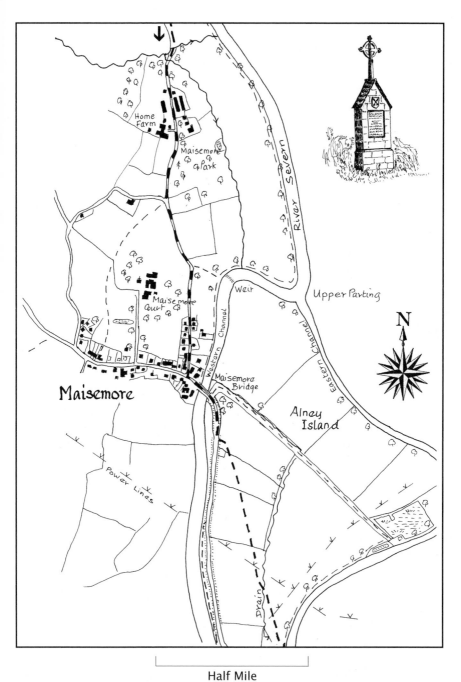

Home Farm

Maisemore Park

River Severn

Maisemore Court

Weir

Upper Parting

Western Channel

Eastern Channel

N

Maisemore Bridge

Maisemore

Alney Island

Power Lines

Drain

Half Mile

Reproduced by kind permission of Ordnance Survey © Crown Copyright MC/99-073

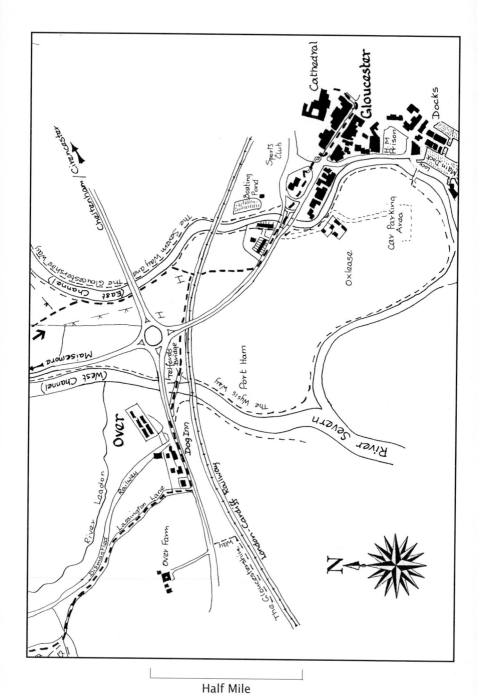

Half Mile

Reproduced by kind permission of Ordnance Survey © Crown Copyright MC/99-073

Mileages

Tibberton	6	6
Cliffords Mesne	4.4	10.4
Kilcot	**2**	**12.4**
Marcle	5.2	17.6
Sleaves Oak	3.2	20.8
Woolhope	2	22.8
Haugh Wood	**2.4**	**25.2**
Mordiford	1.2	26.4
Hereford Cathedral	4.4	30.8
Lugwardine	3.2	34
Withington	**2.8**	**36.8**
Ocle Pychard	3.6	40.4
Much Cowarne	2	42.4
Munderfield Row	5.6	48
Stanford Bishop	**2.4**	**50.4**
Suckley Knowl	3.2	53.7
Knightwick	2.8	56.5
Broadgreen	4	60.5
Broadheath	**2.8**	**63.3**
Worcester Cathedral	3.2	66.5
Timberline Bridge	2	68.5
Stanbrook	2	70.5
Old Hills	1.5	72
Madresfield	2	74
Malvern Link Common	**1.5**	**75.5**
Wyche Cutting	3.5	79
British Camp	2.4	81.4
Hollybush	2.4	83.8
Pendock	**4.8**	**88.6**
Lowbands	1.2	89.8
Staunton	2	91.8
Ashleworth	3.2	95
Maisemore	3.2	98.2
Gloucester Cathedral	**2.4**	**100.6**

Tourist Information Centres

28 Southgate Street,
GLOUCESTER.
01452 421188

7 Church Street,
NEWENT.
01531 822468

3 The Homend,
LEDBURY.
01531 636147

Edde Cross Street,
ROSS ON WYE
01989 562768

1 King Street,
HEREFORD.
01432 268430

1 Rowberry Street,
BROMYARD,
01885 482038

The Guildhall,
High Street,
WORCESTER.
01905 726311

21 Church Street,
MALVERN.
01684 892289

4 High Street,
UPTON ON SEVERN.
01684 594200

The Museum,
64 Barton Street,
TEWKESBURY.
01684 295027

NOTES

NOTES